Don't JUST Retire and Die

A new approach to your life and work after 40

By Craig Nathanson

Copyright © 2009 Craig Nathanson
Craig Nathanson – The Vocational Coach™

All rights reserved. No part of this publication may be reproduced, stored in a retrieval system or transmitted, in any form or by any means, without prior written permission from the author.

Dr. Craig Nathanson
PO Box 2823
Petaluma Ca 94953
Phone 707-774-6446
www.drcraignathanson.com
craignathanson@gmail.com

Layout and design: Anita Flegg and Sigrid Macdonald
Editing: Anita Flegg
Proofreading and Layout: Sigrid Macdonald
Cover art: Robyn Kralik

Nathanson, Craig, 1956 –
    Don't Just Retire and Die / Craig Nathanson

ISBN: 978-0-578-01441-8

    1. Mid-life vocation 2. Vocational happiness 3. Self-help

Table of Contents

Dedication   9

Introduction   11

Purpose   13
    Who are you? 13
    Is your life's purpose for sale? 14
    Is your work full of purpose? 18
  Craig B. conquers despair   21

Prize   25
    What do you cherish most in life? 25
    What do you prize most in mid-life? 26
  What is most important to you?   31
  Marketing executive becomes the Reading Doctor   35

Perspective   39
    How do you view yourself and the world around you? 39
    How to redefine success through your work and life?..40
    Adjust your plan as you go 43
    How do you feel about yourself? 48
  Software engineer becomes coffee house owner   52
  Colleen, motivated and motivational   54

Possibilities   59
    What is possible for you? 59
    What is possible? 60
    Ask yourself new questions 63
  Corporate manager turns to video production   67
  Occupational therapist answers the call   69

Place   73
    What is your role in the world? 73

  Why people ignore their inner needs at mid-life 74
  Why does it take so long to decide to change? 74
  Does finding my place in the world require change? ...78
 Engineer turned author helps others   82
 From mid-life to pet-sitting in Dublin, Ireland 84

Position   89
  What is your attitude on a daily basis? 89
  What is your attitude towards your work?....................90
 Kevin — beyond "the Wall"   95

Passion   101
  How can I find it and keep it?.......................................101
  How do you discover and live your passion? 102
  Make your passions work for you................................107
 Sales exec finds passion in a nonprofit 111
 Writer Robin follows her passion   113

Perfect Vocational Day   117
  How to discover and experience it..............................117
  Envision and live your perfect vocational day............118
  Turning work into vocation 125
  Twenty secrets for finding your perfect work.............128
 Rosemary bounces back   131

Present   135
  Closing the gap between where you are and what you want..135
  What to do right now 136
  The difference between "need" and "want".................140
  Where do you want to contribute? 144
  Economic crisis: what to do about it............................149
  Your life depends on it...154
  Five steps to move to what you want most 158
  The top 10 ways to quit your job 163

Mid-life Monica picked up a paintbrush	168

Permission — 173
- Look for the defining moments in your life 173
- The top 10 FATAL mistakes after 40 174
- The next 10 steps to save your life 177
- How you can live an authentic life 181
- How to build the support network you'll need 182
- Give yourself permission now to follow your heart ... 186
- The Booklet Queen and new fulfillment — 190
- The Art Coach meets the Vocational Coach — 193

Putting it all together — 197
- How can I live a more fulfilling life? 197
- Is this your story, too? — 202
  - A better way 204
  - Taking that first step helps……................................. 205

Final thoughts — 207

References and resources — 209
- Craig's biography — 213

Dedication

This book is dedicated to my wife, Natasha Nathanson, who provides so much unconditional love on this path of living an authentic life. To my children, Nicole, Justin, Nastia, and Chad, who provide daily reminders of the joy having family to love and care for brings.

This book is also dedicated to the many clients I have had the honor of working with over the years. Your stories keep me inspired for the work I do.

Also, a special dedication to Dr. John Beebe, who taught me the importance of integrity, and to Dr. Jeremy Shapiro, who taught me how to think like a scholar and not lose my sense of self throughout my doctoral studies.

To my editor and good friend, Anita Flegg, whose creative support and editing expertise helped make this project a reality.

I am also grateful to my loyal assistant, Ajish Kumar, for his dedication, commitment, and belief in my work while handling all my daily administrative duties with passion and purpose.

Lastly, to my artist, Robyn Kralik, who took the vision for my life's work and created the art for the cover and theme of this book — I am inspired.

Introduction

This book was written in a year of financial turmoil in which millions of people around the world have seen their retirement nest eggs shrink, and their houses decrease in value. For many, a generalized anxiety about their future keeps them up at night.

While I can appreciate this current state, in many ways this panic is self-induced by our society. I have never understood the concept of investing for the future when the present isn't providing a joyful and fulfilling life.

An unhappy and unfulfilling life is the current state for millions of Americans, and according to my research, this proves true for most people over forty when it comes to work.

The majority of people just wait out their work years, until the time when their investments are big enough for them to finally retire, so they can do something else. The problem with this strategy, as we've seen in the economic crisis of 2008 and 2009, is that life gets in the way.

Retirement is no longer an idea that makes sense. People are living longer, in many cases well into their eighties, and the idea of simply retiring twenty, or even thirty, years earlier no longer makes sense. We have the word "retire" thanks to the French, and it originally meant to "slow down" or "crawl under." That is the last thing people want to do in mid-life.

As I write this book, I am fifty-two years old, and I feel like I am thirty-two. I have more energy now than I did in my younger years, and I have many projects planned. The thought of stopping my work feels no different to me than the thought of dying. And this is exactly what happens to most people when they stop working. They grow old and bored quickly, which leads to a focus on the past, followed by death.

The idea I present in this book is that at mid-life, we should stop working at "just a job," and starting living an authentic life.

In 2001, I trademarked the term "vocational passion." What I mean by vocational passion is to live your vocation doing work that aligns with your abilities and interests.

Vocation is work that is joyful, coherent with your integrity, and that provides meaning to your life. Vocation is work that never stops until you stop breathing.

I hope this book inspires you to discover and live your vocational passion now. Your best long term investment is to do work that fits you "just right." As I wrote in my first book, *P Is for Perfect: Your Perfect Vocational Day,* and my second book, *How to Discover and Live Your Passion 365 Days a Year*, you can begin to take charge of your life and your work now, and stop waiting for Someday to come.

I hope this book serves as a guide to inspire you, nudge you, and change your thinking about your work and your life. I am proud to showcase the stories of others who have taken this journey — you can, too. Remember, I'll be cheering you on as you go!

— Craig Nathanson, February 2009

Purpose

Who are you?

What is your life about? How will you make a difference in the world?

How do you most want to make a contribution in the world at this point in your life?

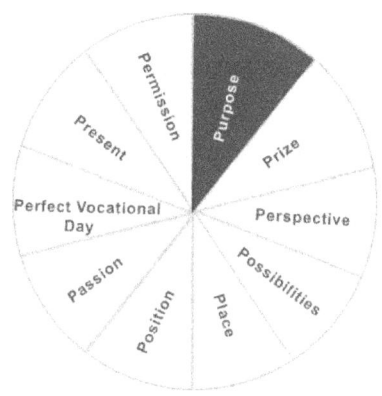

Your purpose drives your behavior and can provide you with daily energy and a sense of doing what is just right for you. What is the purpose of your life?

Mid-life adults with purpose can experience:

- a greater sense of integrity and authenticity
- an experience of being more alive
- an increased feeling of contribution
- stronger health and psychological well-being
- a life that's more congruent
- an acceptance of your own mortality and as a result, less fear of death and a greater sense of your life plans and their meaning

- a feeling of greater control over your life, and a feeling that your life matters
- increased self-esteem and happiness

Is this enough incentive for you?

You can discover and live a more purposeful life. Don't simply surrender to a world that will continue to rent your skills to suit its purposes. A greater second half is possible if you take action now.

Is your life's purpose for sale?

There is no purpose too big or too small

Meet Joe. He's a bridge toll-taker in the San Francisco Bay area. In a recent interview, Joe said he loves the role he has filled for the last twelve years. The job suits his purpose. He said, "If I can help someone start their day off right in the few seconds when they are handing me [the toll], I feel I have made a difference in the day and life of another person."

Meet Mel. He's a veteran New York City street sweeper who works through the night clearing away the previous day's debris. I ran into Mel one morning after my run in Central Park. Mel said, "Nothing makes me happier than making sure no one has to step on garbage when they start out their day on *my* street." He has been sweeping the same four square city blocks for thirty years.

Meet Minna Valentine, a.k.a. "The Reading Doctor." A past client of Craig's, she's a former marketing executive who ditched the corporate world to teach English as a Second Language. This is her take on the changes she made in her vocational path: "Teaching others makes me feel like I am contributing to something worthwhile."

Joe, Mel, and Minna each go to work every day knowing they will make a difference to someone. They are grateful to be able to do so. There are many so-called high-achievers earning six-figure salaries that cannot make that claim.

Why is living with purpose critical in mid-life?

In mid-life, many people find themselves suddenly questioning everything — careers, lifestyles, and priorities. Nothing is spared from this examination, although very few people will discuss their fears.

Often it takes a personal crisis — a layoff, a death, or a divorce — to move people from introspection to action. These events open up a small window of opportunity to challenge everything, and consider a new course.

Inner questioning is critical in mid-life. If a person hopes to achieve greater meaning and fulfillment, things are never easy. It requires courage and a leap of faith.

I speak from experience. Some years ago, I came home from my six-figure job and announced to my family that I was quitting. I no longer found meaning and fulfillment in what I was doing. That was my first leap of faith.

How do I find and live with purpose?

Finding the meaning of life is not self-indulgent or cliché. It is the essence of why we are here on earth. If there is no meaning, then what is the point of our existence? To create a path toward meaning, in our jobs and in our lives, we need to begin with an evaluation process that challenges what we think and how we live.

Start by answering these questions for yourself:

- Fill in the blank:

    "The purpose of my life is _____."
    Keep saying it until you find an answer. Then write it down.

- Make an honest assessment of your current state. Ignore any external input or validation. Are you driven? Are you a procrastinator? Are you happy? Sad? Energetic? Lethargic? Generous? Selfish? Adventurous? Conservative? Write down the words you would use to describe how you are feeling and behaving today.

- Define the experiences you need now to feel fully alive. Then develop a plan to have those experiences. Do you want to travel to China before you turn fifty? Have you always wanted to sing in front of a large audience? Have you always wanted to study to become a chef? Have you always wanted to run a marathon? Fill in your own dreams.

- Define exactly what you're passionate about and where you want to make a contribution. Is it music? Teaching? Sports? Photography? Cooking? Academics? Write down the thing or things that bring out the spark in you.

- Define what is most important to you. Then set short and long-term goals that align with these priorities. Without a clear path, goals are mere daydreams. Set up a process to monitor your progress.

- Define the new experiences that you must have to add a greater sense of meaning and fulfillment to your life. Do you need to start cooking more? Traveling? Taking classes? Skydiving? Make your own list, and write it down.
- Define your beliefs about yourself. Then, change the beliefs that are no longer useful to you. Do you believe you deserve to do what you love? Or do you believe that work is not meant to be fun and meaningful?

Dr. James Hollis, a scholar on philosopher Carl Jung, and a writer about mid-life issues, said that as we grow older, meaning and purpose become equal in importance. We need both to thrive. Carl Jung wrote that, early in life, meaning is derived through preparation for living. In later years, meaning is derived through an examination of the inner self.

What are the results of living with purpose in mid-life?

Victor Frankl, a Nazi death camp survivor, believed that the urge of human beings to search for meaning is inborn. Researcher Martin Bolt said that having meaning and a defined purpose in life makes it possible to accept our own mortality with less fear of death, and a greater sense of life's plans and their meaning.

Is this enough incentive for you?

You can discover and live a more purposeful life now. Don't simply surrender to a world that will continue to rent your skills to suit its purposes. A greater second half is possible if you take action now.

Is your work full of purpose?

How do you define your work?
Do you look to your work to define meaning and joy or just to collect a paycheck? Each of these carries a different result. Those who seek meaning and joy in their work tend to choose carefully what they do; they know what they do helps determine who they are. For those who work just for the money, there is little expectation of meaning or joy — just as long as the paycheck rolls in.

Career vs. vocational passion
In my work, I am often asked, "What is the difference between a career and vocational passion?"

Jobs are just an exchange of services for money. Careers are the same but with a better title.

Sadly, for many people,
jobs=careers=retirement=death.

Can you avoid death?

Probably not, but you can get more enjoyment and happiness out of each and every day before you get there.

Vocational passion means having a life's work that you can do for your whole lifetime without the need to ever retire.

Retirement is only for people who don't like what they do
Want a quick path to death? Retire and wait.

Sure, there's much to do including travel, relaxing, and visiting friends, but this doesn't last long. For most of us, our later years will also bring tension and anxiety about how to spend our days, and in many cases, how to make a contribution.

Are you on a path to just retire, too?

The word "retire" comes from the French word meaning "retreat," "take out of circulation," "move away from," "withdraw from," and "rest."

Is this what you want for the second half of your life?

Here's the best way to retire and then die.
- Worry about what others will think if you start to do what you love.
- Look for approval from others.
- Be afraid of change.
- Wait for a crisis to occur.

What happens in mid-life?

We reevaluate everything from our relationships, our work, our health, our finances, and our emotional state. We need to recognize that this is healthy and important to do.

Gain purpose in your life now

Realize that what you do determines who you are. Is your work a reflection of who you are and who you want to be?

Mid-life is a great time to:
- Align your abilities and your interests.
- Reflect deeply about what you are passionate about.
- Ensure your work is maximally expressive of your passions.

- Ensure your work meets your personal needs.
- Ensure that the work you do feels just right for you.

Craig B. conquers despair

Craig Barton struggled with his *vocation* his whole life. While he hung in there and usually made decent money, he often asked himself, "Why am I so unhappy?"

Craig was proud that he was able to support his wife and three children on a job based 100% on commission. Craig's family always had anything they wanted, but Craig was miserable on the inside. He didn't realize that misery on the inside was manifesting to the outside, slowly, but surely, and one day his wife told him that she wanted a divorce. Craig was shocked and absolutely devastated.

Within one month of that news, he learned that his friend, and owner of the company he worked for, was dying of a brain tumor.

Craig's back was against the wall; he was suicidal. All he could think was, "I can't kill myself; I have three kids." It was a struggle to do even simple things like laundry.

The first thing Craig did was to take a local job (that he hated) just to be around people. He searched the Internet every day reaching for anybody that might be able to help him. The pain was so intense, Craig can still remember many specific situations vividly.

He still remembers the negative words he was using, and learning how to reframe them. Being a salesman, Craig Barton knew all about reframing, and he realized that he had better work on reframing his inner man. He thought he was a strong man of faith, but he was coming very close to losing that, too. He needed a new purpose in his life to focus on, and he turned to real estate — something he really loved.

With new purpose and energy, Craig felt he couldn't lose. He worked on real estate, and on his soul, every day. He reframed and believed to the extent that, if this didn't work, he would surely have been completely devastated. It was frightening, but Craig was overcoming his fears through the strength he was gaining in his soul.

Things started to happen, and Craig would often get a deal going at just the right time. Even though he had deals working, the money wasn't coming in fast enough. Living on credit cards was a challenge, but Craig knew his faith would not be denied.

Then it happened — a deal closed here, and a deal closed there — and boom: his credit cards were paid off and Craig had money in the bank.

Craig now knows he has a great life ahead of him. Even though we sometimes go through incredible pain, we all need to remember we have so much to be thankful for.

Lessons to learn

What can we learn from Craig Barton's story?

When you have faith in yourself and others, magical things can happen in your life, despite the odds!

It is easy to become overwhelmed when life's challenges hit after forty. As in Craig's case, life can suddenly feel like a game that is just too difficult to play.

Suddenly everything Craig had come to define as success was crumbling around him. This happens to many people. It can feel so overwhelming, some people decide to give up. The problem with this strategy is that there is no one who will come to the rescue. It takes a new strategy, one that may go against society's expectations of success or what you have been taught.

It is only when redefining what success after forty really means, and learning new ways of measuring success, that your authentic life filled with purpose can emerge.

It will not come all at once, but in pieces. One day you feel a little lighter on your feet, the next day new ideas emerge, and suddenly you realize your life is in your control and determined by your feelings, actions, and your desired direction.

Craig's story teaches us a valuable lesson. Taking the time to reflect deeply about your needs and desires after forty is not only important for finding purpose, it is mandatory.

With a new sense of purpose you can start to lead a life that allows you to give back. You learn that you really do control more of your life than you are led to believe. Only then will your natural gifts and talents start to emerge, and your life will never be the same.

Life will be richer and deeper, and you will live it with more awareness.

What is the purpose of your life? There can be no question more important after we turn forty.

Prize

What do you cherish most in life?

What is most important to you? What behaviors would you have to follow each day to be true to yourself?

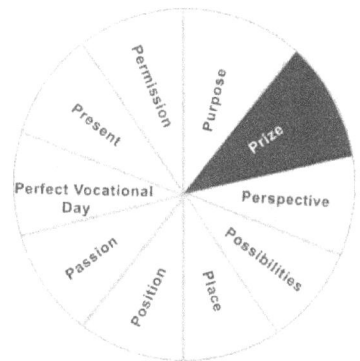

What would you have to do each day to *not* follow what is most important to you?

Are you working in a job that has nothing to do with what you prize most in life?

It is critical to identify what is most important to you. It is just as critical to know what you would have to do to follow — or not follow — each day what is most important to you.

It can be helpful to prioritize the three to five elements that you prize most. This can help you to set new goals around what is most important to you.

The most important thing is not to surrender to what you think should be most important based on either society's desire or those who love you. Your list must be based on what — right now — is most important to you. Be honest and open. Your list will give you clarity and the start to an authentic life.

What do you prize most in mid-life?

A key ingredient of happiness is finding vocational passion. This is the message people in mid-life most need to hear. Finding the perfect alignment of interests and abilities can make going to work seem like it isn't work at all. People who find the magic balance tend to be healthier and more energetic, and they find more satisfaction in other areas of their lives, too.

Too many people go through life without having their interests and abilities aligned. The inevitable result is a feeling of deep ennui as people drag themselves out of bed every day to endure the grind required to support the lifestyles of their families. You may do your job well, even exceptionally well. But the work itself is rarely what propels you. Instead, it's a sense of obligation or a feeling of being trapped.

But there is another way. You can develop a plan to escape the grind, and then find work that means something to you. Once you do that, you can build a comfortable lifestyle around it.

Too many people allow their lifestyles (or the lifestyles they are conditioned to expect) to dictate the kind of work they do. And that is where so many people get into trouble, both spiritually and financially.

I discovered all of this the hard way. Now, my mission is to take what I've learned and help others as they transition into their vocational passion.

Making the transition requires courage, risk-taking, and a willingness to make significant personal changes. But with determination and planning, anyone can do it. You will ask yourself later why you waited so long.

Wake up to the rest of your life

I had a good job, a million-dollar house, and a great family. I also had staggering personal debt from leading a materialistic lifestyle. To top it off, I found no satisfaction in my work. My way out came suddenly.

Eight years ago, I had an epiphany as I stood before my co-workers, giving yet another slide presentation. I suddenly shut down. I realized that I couldn't do it anymore. I stopped where I was, and went home.

I woke up the next morning and felt more or less back to my old self. *Perhaps they were right*, I thought. *Maybe I just had a touch of the flu.* So I drove to work. But when I got to the parking lot, I couldn't get out of the car.

In spite of this wakeup call, I didn't take the final plunge right away. I felt too tied to the life I was living. So I struggled through other jobs over the next few years, but the results and feelings were the same.

Finally, I had had enough. I still had the responsibility of being the sole provider for my wife and three children. We had a big mortgage, we were caring for a seriously ill child, dealing with growing medical bills, and struggling under $200,000 in credit card debt.

In the middle of a tough economy, I walked away from a six-figure job as vice president and managing director of a billion-dollar multinational firm.

This time, there was no turning back.

I had no intention of walking away from my responsibilities. But I had to find a way to earn my income in a more meaningful way. Today, I have a private coaching practice, a busy speaking schedule, and over forty products all focused on helping others in mid-life discover and do what they love.

Every day in my practice, I see people who are having the same emotional, professional, financial, and relationship challenges that I went through.

It wasn't easy getting here. The first few years were extremely painful. Financial stress increased, relationships were strained, and emotional stress reached all-time highs. But now, eight years later, I have emerged with a more congruent and authentic life.

I can say with confidence that it has all been worth it.

What matters to you?

If you want to find your vocational passion, it has to begin with a question: "What is most important to me?"

This may be the most important question you will ever ask yourself. You need to look deep inside yourself to turn your vague longings into tangible goals, with real paths toward achieving them.

Once you answer the question and see the path the answers light for you, then it's time to summon the courage to make the transition.

Matt Vande Voorde walked away from an executive position at a large bank to follow what he prized most in his life. His dream was to publish a magazine that helps people with disabilities use the Internet. Today, Matt is the proud publisher of Accessible Content Magazine.

Jim Goebelbecker was tired of long hours selling products he didn't care about. He prized his family and nonprofit work. He took a risk and never looked back. Today, Jim is an executive with a large nonprofit organization on the east coast. He works just ten minutes away from his home.

Five steps to discover and follow your passion

Making this level of change in your life isn't an overnight process. Once you understand that a change is essential to making the rest of your life matter, you can follow these five steps to transform your dreams and desires into concrete actions.

1. Evaluate what you want. Ask the big questions and answer them honestly. (Why lie to yourself?)

2. Envision your future. You need to visualize what you're dreaming about. Then develop a concrete understanding of what it will take to get there.

3. Tune out negative feedback. Everyone will try to talk you out of making big changes. Listen to yourself, instead.

4. Assess your risks. Take an inventory of your assets, obligations, and health. Then, make the necessary adjustments that will minimize

the impact and risk of making a major life change.

5. Take small steps. You don't have to quit your job tomorrow. You can start in small ways by doing research on your dream vocation, maybe taking a class. Or you can make small lifestyle changes to reduce your personal money "burn rate."

In the end, you must give yourself permission to follow your heart. That's what I did. So did Matt and Jim, and so many others. And like me, they now jump out of bed each morning looking forward to a day of vocational passion. You can have this feeling, too. First, you must decide what's really most important to you.

What is most important to you?

I doubt that anyone will run up to you on Monday morning at work and ask you what is most important to you. Organizational life is concerned with productivity, revenue, and efficiency. What's most important to you and your life is of little value or concern in the organization.

What do you do?

You need to figure out what you do. Start with a deep analysis of who you are and what is most important to you. Since most of your waking days are spent working, what you do will determine who you are.

What work is most important to you?

What is the work that fits you best? What is the work that best aligns your abilities and your interests?

What kind of work gives you fulfillment and meaning?

This is another question no one will ask you at your job today. You need to figure this out for yourself.

What kind of work culture fits you best?

Do you want to teach? Then work around teachers.

Do you want to design? Then work around engineers.

Do you want to build? Then work around builders.

Design an environment to fit you

Many studies have shown that the best work environments include fresh air, windows, soft colors, individualized music, climate controls, cushy chairs, and so on.

So why do we spend our lives in gray cubicles with walls that can't even support hanging pictures of our loved ones? Windows and fresh air are nowhere to be found, or if they are, they have to be earned.

Do you yearn to work in a big building in the city or a small cottage in the country? Do you want to work inside or outdoors? Do you want to work by yourself, with a small group of people, or with a large group? Are you an early riser or do you prefer to ease into your day?

Make a list

Start by listing the details that are most important to you in your life.

Write down how you will know when you are following what is most important to you, and how you will know when you're not. With this list in mind, you can begin to design short and long term goals that align with what is most important to you.

Your work determines who you are

So many people that come to me are stuck in a vocational rut. They soon discover that the work they have been doing all their lives no longer fits their self-image and what is most important to them.

I had a friend once who was an artist. He took a day job processing paperwork for an insurance firm to pay the rent. He told me later he came home too exhausted to paint.

He suddenly realized one day that he had become an insurance clerk.

So many possibilities for you

There are so many possibilities for you. What bothers you most about the world? What would you like to change? What change do you most want to see in the world, your country, your city, your neighborhood?

You can do the work best suited to making changes you want to see, but you must start thinking in new possibilities.

What is possible right now?

As you think about the work you are most passionate about, what is possible right now? Be careful — your life is determined by what you do.

Your happiness and your self-worth affect the quality of your life each and every day.

There are no shortcuts to vocational passion.

Retirement is the biggest myth of all

The only people who retire are those who don't love what they do. If you did what you loved each and every day, why would you ever want to stop?

Mid-life is a time to narrow the choices

With the best part of your life remaining, now is the time to focus on what is truly most important to you and what work you are most passionate about.

There is no time to waste.

After forty, there is a greater sense of the passage of time and the need to make the best use of it. You have no time to waste on activities that have no meaning for you, especially in your work.

What about the money?

No more excuses. You have a choice right now. You can fill your days with work that lacks meaning and happiness or you can decide *now* to close the gap between what you are doing now and the work you are most passionate about.

Life can be rich without money

To truly experience a rich life, you must decide to focus on what is most important to you and take action to move towards it.

The six steps to reach your goal are:

1. Envision it.
2. Write it down.
3. Talk to others about it.
4. Take small steps daily towards doing what you love.
5. Measure your progress and make adjustments to your path as you go.
6. Reward yourself daily.

Your life is a journey

Take the path that seems most interesting, most fun, and most meaningful and you'll never look back. You will live a richer life and become a wonderful role model for others.

Marketing executive becomes the Reading Doctor

Minna started out working for an advertising agency in New York City. She was very interested in what motivates people to take action. A move to Atlanta, and her job working on accounts such as Burger King and Coca-Cola, provided her with the opportunity to explore this area.

However, after a marriage and divorce, she felt the need to do something more to feel valued. She became a literacy tutor and, in her spare time, helped several adults to learn to read. When dotcom fever swept the country, she switched careers and became a senior VP of Marketing for a Louisville software company that delivered solutions for advertising agencies.

She enjoyed her position but still wanted to do more, so she continued her volunteer tutoring. Six years later, the company was sold to a California start-up and she found herself without a job. Although she tried consulting for several months, she decided that it wasn't for her. And, at the same time, she came to the realization that she did not want to live in Louisville any longer.

Minna moved to Northern California and got another software marketing job, this time as an alliance director — "job" is the operative word. She made an excellent salary and performed well, but she didn't feel fulfilled. She didn't look forward to going to work, and she was relieved when the work week was over and she could just stay home.

After exactly one year, she was laid off and began, once again, to look for another job. She had several interviews but she couldn't get excited about any of the openings she found, and she really didn't want to work at any of the companies she spoke with. But she liked the idea of earning big money once again, so she kept on interviewing.

Suddenly, Minna's father died. This event made Minna realize that you can't predict what will happen or how much time is left to each of us. If she wanted to do something that would make her happy and bring her satisfaction, she'd better start doing it. She had no idea what she really wanted to do or how to figure it out.

One day she heard me speak at a networking meeting, and something I said struck a chord. I wasn't preaching an esoteric philosophy or suggesting unrealistic goals. I was merely encouraging the audience to figure out what made them most happy and then to try to find a way to incorporate that into their everyday work. She contacted me and began a long process of figuring out what she *prized* most in her life, and what would make her happy.

With my help, she finally realized that her tutoring experience provided the perfect springboard for a career switch. Minna got her California teaching credentials and began teaching English as a Second Language at three adult schools in Silicon Valley.

She also started The Reading Doctor, a coaching service dedicated to "improving communication skills, one word at a time."

So far, the money's not great but every time she walks into a classroom or helps someone learn to read, she feels an immediate gratification and a sense of accomplishment. She looks forward to going to work and enjoys every day.

Lessons to learn

What can we learn from Minna's story?

Once you figure out what is most important to you, it takes a decision and action to move towards doing more of what you love in your vocational life. This can be challenging if you have fallen into a pattern of doing what you have always been good at.

After forty it is much better to follow a path of your passions and interests, and learn as you go, rather than continue down a road of doing work you are no longer interested in.

Minna's story teaches us that a new vocational path takes small steps. These steps can start from a simple new idea. This idea only comes from deep thought and the realization that what you are doing is no longer working. In fact, a deeper self-awareness brings new insight that your life doesn't fit anymore. As with those six year-old jeans still hanging in the closet, you need to make an effort to throw away the old. Only after the old is discarded do new possibilities emerge.

After forty, it is important to examine your abilities and interests, and focus where the alignment is just perfect. This can bring fulfillment, joy, and meaning back to your life.

Again, this must be a solo exercise; you must be free of external views and opinions.

Minna's story also teaches us that sometimes it takes trial and error before your life starts to work just right. Be patient with yourself while starting down the road to insight and self-discovery. With each new step, small pieces of evidence will emerge that this new life built around what you prize can actually work.

After forty, it is mandatory to be selfish about your life and work. Only then can a life of integrity and authenticity emerge.

Perspective

How do you view yourself and the world around you?

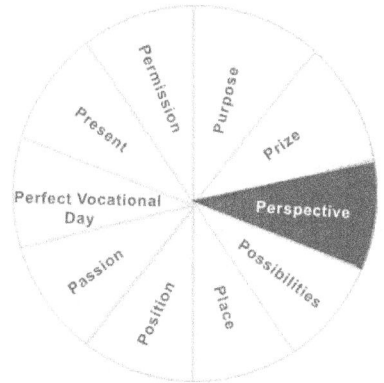

Many people have views about your capabilities, what you should do, who you should be, and where you need improvement.

What's more important is the perspective you have of yourself. Remember, you can change anything that's not useful to you any longer.

What is your perspective of the world? This can affect how you engage in a way that either treats the world as dangerous, or a place full of potential and possibilities.

A healthy perspective will make you feel better, and you will feel better about others as well.

How to redefine success through your work and life?

How do you define success?
If you are like most people, your definition of success is based on external factors. A nice house, perfect children, a trophy wife or husband, nice vacations, lots of material things, and of course, a great big salary.

What price will you pay for external success?
This is a question worth thinking about. Are you willing to work ten, fifteen, or twenty-five years at "just a job" that you don't really enjoy? Will all those material things make a miserable work life worth it in the end? Will you even have time to enjoy these things? Certainly, your family will enjoy these things. Is that enough to make it worth you spending all those years doing meaningless work?

Do you need the approval of others?
Many of us will work for many years at something we dislike, for the approval of others. Your mother-in-law is proud, and your wife or husband brags about your job title at social gatherings. Does this make it worth it?

There are tradeoffs
As a public speaker, author, and coach whose life mission is to help people discover and do what they love, I can tell you there are tradeoffs.

People over forty usually know, deep inside, that their twenty years of working have met external society standards, but in many cases have not met their internal need for joy in their work.

As a college professor, I have taught thousands of students who are very focused on grades and making lots of money, but who have not been taught how to figure out exactly what work fits them best.

Both age groups, the over-forties and the students, are often confused, scared, and lost.

Define success from the inside out

First, you must have a vision of what you want. What work excites you? Is there someone you envy — someone who does similar work? If you had fifty million dollars, what work would you do right now?

Next, write down what you want. It's amazing what happens when you actually write it down. In many ways, it forces you to see your dream from a new perspective. Try it now for yourself.

Write down the work you really want to do.

You might write something like:

The work I really want to do is _____
because _____.

I have found, in my research and in my experience, that when we know the reasons *why* we want something, then we can start to move towards it.

Talk to others about your plans

Many people stop short of their dreams by not talking about what they want. It almost doesn't matter who you talk to, as long as you discuss your plans with others.

They will, of course, offer their opinions; ignore them. You are simply sharing what you have already decided to do.

Take small steps

Every success in life starts with a small step.

Let's say you have a vision of yourself as a high school history teacher.

You have written down that you plan to become a teacher because this is something you enjoy, and because you believe you could make a difference in the lives of your students.

Now you start to tell people your plans. By doing this, you actually start to commit these plans to yourself, and it will be hard to turn back. You call a local school, and set up a meeting with a high school history teacher to find out exactly what you have to do next. Then you call and have a college send you enrolment papers to start a program to get the credentials you need. Now there is no turning back.

Now measure your steps

Now that you have committed to your new life, you'll have to measure your steps. First, talk to your family, and come up with a plan to accommodate the new life you are working towards. You may have to adjust your standard of living, or maybe just pay more attention to your spending.

Start measuring your progress towards your goal, and plan where you will focus next.

Learn to celebrate

You will be disappointed if you wait for a family member, or anyone else, to reward your progress.

The rewards will have to come from you. I have learned that, when a person starts to live a life of integrity, this is often reward enough.

You no longer have to compare yourself to others. It no longer matters who has the better house or car or spouse.

Adjust your plan as you go

As you make progress towards your new goals, and learn more about your chosen field, you will continually adjust your vision to the reality you seek.

How do you define success?

When you define success as a contest to help you keep up with the new toys others have, you will always lose. There will always be someone new to compete with.

But when you do the work you love, and that fits you, you will be happy and content inside, and just grateful that you have found your own authentic path. This is the best reward of all.

Now you will start to appreciate others without the need to compete.

Live to your own standards by starting to move towards doing the work you love. It will not always be easy, but it will be worth it.

How do you view yourself and the world around you?

What is your perspective about you? How do you feel about you? What is your perspective about the world around you? Your perspective can assist you, or hinder you from reaching your vocational goals in life.

For the purposes of my coaching model, I have defined perspective as the way you think about the world and those around you.

It is easy to believe the perspectives that others have of us, or want us to have about ourselves. Perspectives that were given to us when we were young can stay with us for a long time. Some of our earliest experiences drive our belief systems.

When I was about ten years old, I started running. I was a small kid, and although I enjoyed other sports, running seemed to even things out for me against all those bigger kids.

When I was in ninth grade, I went undefeated in the 330 yard dash. It seemed that in every race I just knew I wouldn't lose. I can remember the championship race at Kezar Stadium where for many years the 49ers football team played.

As I stood in lane one and looked at all those bigger kids lined up ahead of me in their lanes, I had the perspective that all I had to do was run my race and everything would work out. There must have been a few thousand people in the stands, including my grandfather and grandmother. When the gun went off, it seemed that all the other kids immediately got off to a big lead. Halfway around the track, I was in last place. I can remember the feeling even now, almost forty years later. I just knew I would be fine if I listened to my pace and did what I knew I could do. As I rounded the final turn, I picked up the pace and started to pass the kids one by one. With fifty yards to go, there was one very big kid in front of me. He had a ten-yard lead and it didn't look good. I can remember saying to myself, "I can catch him."

With ten yards to go, I found an extra gear I didn't know I had, and with one last kick, I passed the last big kid and won the city championship.

Four years later, in my senior year in high school, I went undefeated in my cross-country events (long distance running). As I continued to be one of the smallest kids in my class, running became my place to practice belief. Again, in every race that year, as I stood at the starting line, I just knew I wouldn't lose. In the championship race at another historic place, the Polo Fields in San Francisco's Golden Gate Park, I stood at the starting line again knowing what I needed to do.

As we finished the first mile and exited through the tunnel, the kids from the rival school formed a wall in front of me so I couldn't pass. I didn't panic. I believed in myself and what I was capable of. I had mentally rehearsed this race for many months. As the first group reached the top of the hill and rounded the big tree that had stood in the meadow for over sixty years, I made my move. I raced around the kids who suddenly lost their protective wall as they rounded the tree. As I raced by and caught them by surprise, I felt my pace increasing and my arms and legs gaining momentum. I never looked back. As I charged up the final hill, I caught a quick look at my former seventh grade coach who had been following my progress.

He yelled, "Come on, Craig, last hill. You can do this."

Hearing his voice gave me even more confidence.

When you are around other people who support your beliefs and have a positive perspective of you, it adds fuel to your emotional bank account. As I raced through that last tunnel into the darkness that lasted only four or five seconds, it seemed much longer. As I entered that tunnel, it became dark and quiet. I was alone with my thoughts. I could hear my breathing, my feet hitting the ground, and the echo of the tunnel. I exited the tunnel and emerged into the sunlight with the greatest feeling in the world.

That's the feeling you get when you believe in yourself and you can show evidence of that belief.

As I rounded the track and raced home to end another undefeated season as the city champion, I raised my arms in victory as I broke the banner. I looked over and saw lots of people in the stands.

Grandpa was missing — he had died in my arms from cancer the year before. Grandma was home sick, and Mom was working, as always.

In a way, I felt as if my victory proved to myself and to others that much was possible in this world if you started with the perspective that you could do it.

As a footnote to this story, thirty years later I was with my then five year-old son at a craft fair and I noticed an elderly man selling black-and-white photographs.

There, among the hundreds of photos, was a picture of that tunnel, the one I had run through on the way to my victory. I bought the photograph with the same excitement as a child able to spend his whole dollar on candy.

I told my little son this story and he said, "Daddy, would you take me to the tunnel sometime, so I can run with you through it, too?"

Through that exchange with my son, I learned that having a positive perspective about myself could also be something to pass on, to leave behind for others to try out for themselves.

Now it's your turn. What is your perspective about you? Make a list right now of all the things that you believe about you. What are they? Are they helpful? Are they useful? Remember, if you don't like your perspective, you can change it.

Imagine replacing one of the views about yourself that you don't like with one that is more useful. How would that feel? Try it right now. Take a perspective that you aren't especially proud of and change it to a more useful one.

Notice how this feels as you try on this changed perspective like a new shirt. How does it rest within you? How does it fit you? If at first, it doesn't quite fit right, don't worry. You can always have it tailored a bit, and after wearing it for a while, you will find that it will fit fine.

What if you discover that this new perspective is different from what others have always told you? I think that's a good sign that you are on the right track to positive change. Finding the right vocation sometimes means trading in an old set of perspectives that just aren't useful any longer.

My middle son used to trade baseball cards. I asked him once why he turned some in and got new ones. He said, "Dad, don't you get it? These cards are old and not worth much anymore. These new ones are cool."

Maybe the same goes for our perspectives. Trade in the old ones and get some new ones.

I once counseled a man in his early sixties who had just been laid off. He shoved his resume across the desk and asked if I could fix it. As I normally do in this situation, I respectfully moved the resume aside and asked this man exactly what it was that he wanted to do with his life.

He told me that no one had ever asked him that before. He said that for most of his life, his parents had taken care of this for him. Now that they were gone, he had no one left to tell him what he should be doing with his vocational life. He explained to me that when he was ten years old, over fifty years ago, he had loved to paint. At the time, his father told him to drop his love for painting because painting would never provide enough income to support a family. As he always did, he listened to his father; he stopped painting and never touched it again.

In our work together, I gave this man permission to follow his dreams again, and do what made him feel happy and full of passion. In tears, he said he would do that, and he immediately started to describe his plans for opening a studio and making it lucrative.

He told me he could make more money as an engineer, but he doubted he would live much longer to enjoy or spend it.

Is there something in your life you need to give yourself permission to do? Is there a perspective you have about yourself that you would like to change?

It all starts with how you view yourself and the world around you.

How do you feel about yourself?

Does your work enhance your sense of self or does it bring you down? Have you thought about how your work might be impacting your health, your relationships, and your happiness? So many people place their work in a large compartment, as if to keep the rest of their life away from their work — I wish it were that simple.

Your work determines who you are

I went out to eat the other day and I noticed a group of about fifteen people from the same work group out to lunch. It was your typical work lunch — the boss did most of the talking and the people tried hard to pretend they were enjoying themselves.

Really, they just wanted to rush home, put on their pajamas and crawl under their covers. Have you ever felt that way?

Stop looking for another job

Instead of looking for another job, create a life that honors who you are and your gifts to the world.

Write down on a piece of paper, "The way I feel about myself is _____."

Change the parts of your life that are no longer useful to you.

So many of us are held prisoner by others — our bosses, our parents, our spouses, and society — about who we should be and the role we should play in life.

Remember, you are the only one who can change the role in your own one-act play called Life. It doesn't come from thinking you should change or hoping for some better luck. It comes from creating the life that works just right for you.

Your work is the center-point of your life. Last week I met an executive whose company sold electronic parts. I asked him if he loved his work and all his travel. He said he actually didn't like it at all. His plan was to someday spend his time in the mountains doing something around his love of skiing. I knew what the real problem was. He lived a life of big screen TVs, large trophy cars, and lots of toys. He couldn't actually imagine giving up any of these in trade for his dreams.

Don't prostitute yourself to your work

I am sorry to say it this way, but it's the best example that comes to mind. So many of us do this. We rent our lives and our souls to faceless work that we perform without question. And the result is that we feel worse about ourselves and who we are.

The path to a life of integrity is an open and honest review of who you are and what you want.

Are you a job title or a person?

When someone asks you what you do, how do you answer?

Do you respond with your job title or a description of who you are?

There are so many jobs out there and most of them would not be done unless people were paid to do them, because they are not fun.

After forty, it's time to take a deeper look at doing work that warms the soul; work that solves real problems in the world.

Is your work making a difference in the world?

Most jobs are created only to help an organization turn a profit. If you can't contribute to this mission, then the organization will find someone else, probably younger, who can.

After forty, you are ready to stop these silly games with your life and find your vocation — the work you will start to do and continue doing until you stop breathing.

Reflection at 52

I am fifty-two years old as I write this book, and I can't think of a better way to start my day. I plan to continue this work for the next forty or fifty years because in some small way, I feel it makes a difference in the world. And along the way it also helps me feel better about myself.

Consider making these your goals, too.

How do you feel about yourself?

Only you can start to take action towards doing something about the answers you don't like. Start by examining your work.

This will be one of the hardest things you will ever do. But it will be very satisfying to look back from the end of your life, and realize you ignored the status quo and followed your heart.

Software engineer becomes coffee house owner

A couple of years ago, during a job interview for an engineering management position, Bonnie Vining was advised not to smile so much. In that instant, she decided to have a new *perspective*. She knew that she wanted a career where a smile would be an asset rather than a liability, and that revelation sparked her idea for Javalina's Coffee and Friends.

She set out on a journey to learn everything she could about specialty coffee and the coffee shop business.

She met some fabulous people along the way, people like Aaron Triplett of Roaster X who has mentored her in every aspect of the specialty coffee business, and Shawn Cole of Chestnut Construction who has set a prime example for outstanding customer service.

She also received tremendous support from lots of people who spent countless hours working on various projects that add unique touches to help make Javalina's special.

Bonnie's hope is that Javalina's will inspire a sense of community on the southeast side of Tucson. She envisions it as a place where employees will stop on their way to work to pick up their first cup of coffee or read the morning paper; a place where stay-at-home moms can get together with their kids in the afternoons; a place where people will meet before a bicycle ride or hike; a place where employees of the nearby shops will enjoy coffee breaks; a place where employees of the University of Arizona Science and Technology Park will gather for meetings, stop by after lunch or for "cappi" hour after work; a place where students will come to study; and an inviting place to bring a date, gather with friends, or use the wireless Internet.

Individuals in the community will shape the character of Javalina's, and she is excited about watching its personality develop over time.

Javalina's will serve specialty coffee drinks, gourmet tea, smoothies, and baked goods with attention to great customer service in an atmosphere that encourages good clean fun. Bonnie looks forward to the whole community becoming a part of Javalina's.

Lessons to learn

Bonnie didn't accept the external perspective on how she should live her life. She decided to have a new perspective about herself and what she wanted to do, and she did it.

This is a wonderful lesson for all of us.

Colleen, motivated and motivational

Married to her better half, Rocky, at the age of nineteen, and then having five children by the age of twenty-six, kept Colleen busy raising their children (and a few others) for many years. She worked off and on in office jobs, along with a few part-time businesses of her own in housekeeping, pet-sitting and beauty product sales.

At age thirty-five, Colleen started college, and she graduated at the age of forty with a Bachelors degree in Accounting. Her career since then has been focused mainly in the business arena, including positions such as Office Administrator, Human Resources Director, Accountant, and currently, Asset and Property Manager for a real estate development company.

Colleen found that she enjoyed smaller entrepreneurial work environments where she could see the effects of her contributions.

Through the years, she noticed that many people were dissatisfied with their lives for any number of reasons. Some just needed a friendly ear to listen to them, or a different perspective to consider. Some needed a cheerleader or coach to help them along.

Though she talked with people of all ages, the concentration of dissatisfaction she noticed was among young adults.

For many years it has been Colleen's belief that we should "think about what we think about," and that our thoughts are the seeds that grow our lives. A new *perspective* (or changing your thoughts about a particular subject or issue) can change your situation, or the way you react to it. She continued to study the writings of many authors in this area, and she attempted her own writing on the subject.

Positive feedback on her efforts came often enough to keep her encouraged that she was on the right track with these beliefs.

A few years ago Colleen became frustrated in her efforts to write motivational material, and she was stalled in developing a plan for moving forward. During this trying period, she became unsure — was this really her true calling? She asked God to take away her desire to teach in this area if it was not His plan for her. Amazingly, He answered instantly, saying, "Who do you think put the desire in your heart? It is already yours. Just reach out and take it." Talk about a confirmation!

Since then, Colleen has changed her approach by thinking a little smaller. She discovered that one of the factors defeating her was that she was trying to take on big projects, when working on smaller projects was more productive. She set up a defined work space, started carving out smaller but more frequent chunks of time for writing, paid more attention to those who were already doing what she wanted to do, and joined Toastmasters International.

Her biggest accomplishment was to let go of her fear and uncertainty about her efforts, and understand that, though there are many others who teach on the same subject, her voice would be unique and it would connect with those who are meant to hear it.

Colleen enjoys her current job, and according to her employer, she does it well, but still job dissatisfaction had crept in over the last year or two.

Fortunately, her employer is very supportive of her motivational speaking efforts, and since she is moving toward her own vocational goals, her job dissatisfaction has disappeared.

"Once I decided to move forward and press on toward my desired vocation, encouragement in many forms has come into my life. A local computer store owner asked me to conduct an employee training session on communication, and I found an encouraging and enthusiastic Toastmasters club. Just last week I met someone from the neighborhood where I grew up, and he said to me, "Have you ever thought of being a motivational speaker? You'd be great at it!"

I replied, "Well, as a matter of fact, I have."

Lessons to learn

Just changing your perspective can give you new direction and energy for a more fulfilling life. Colleen was bored and burned out at work, and she decided to look inside herself. She examined what bothered her most, and what she might do about it. As she became clear about what was most important, she started to gain a new perspective.

With this new perspective she became clearer about what she should do about it. She started with small steps, gained proof for herself, and as a result gained an even clearer view about herself and her work.

So many of us are influenced by others and their views of us. We seek out external opinions first to see if our new choices make sense to others and only then do we venture forward. The sad thing is that it usually takes only a few external perspectives from those not even close to us to shut down our dreams as silly, not achievable, or not worthwhile. Then we go back with our head down to the same old job, hoping for someone to rescue us from job prison.

Instead, armed with a new self-awareness and new dreams, we can venture forward with a new view of ourselves despite what others might think.

If you want to teach, print a business card that says, "Teacher." Carry it around, and start to teach others what you know best, and what you are passionate about. Soon you will reshape a new vision and perspective of your life and your work.

Your life will never be the same!

Possibilities

What is possible for you?

What is possible for you in your vocational life? So many of us instead focus on what's impossible.

What would you have to do to start believing more things are possible for you?

There are many possibilities in the world for each of us, in many areas of our lives.

- vocation
- relationship
- financial
- health and fitness

Most important is how we decide to focus our thinking.

When it comes to vocation, it is often easier to focus on what's impossible rather than what is possible. Our parents, teachers, and friends have told us what we are capable of and often nudged us towards one vocation or another. Many of us fell into our careers by chance instead of by choice.

Take some time to consider what is possible for you right now.

Think about *how* you are going to think about it before you think about it.

Are you thinking about your next steps, or are you thinking about your past, the present, or future work?

Are you thinking about what to do from *your* perspective or from the perspective of another person close to you?

Your mind doesn't know the difference between what is real or imagined when thinking about the future.

Start to think right now about new possibilities for your life and your work

What is possible?

You can create new possibilities and a more meaningful second half of life.

After working in marketing and information technology for thirty years, Dinah Chapman was burned out. She was laid off from her Northern California job in 2004, but rather than wallow in misery, Dinah took the layoff as a blessing. She considered new possibilities, deciding that her life would have more meaning if it centered on her love of music.

Working in a windowless office and selling faceless products brought Justin and Julie Greenberg together. Not only did they discover that they were soul mates, they realized that they were both seeking to create happiness and good energy in their work lives. Justin and Julie, based in Southern California, shared a passion for children and for sports. So they began to think together of new possibilities that eventually turned their love of soccer and kids into their life's work.

There are lots of possibilities in the world for each of us in the areas of vocation, relationships, finances, and health and fitness. What's important is how we decide to focus our thinking in these areas, especially when it comes to our life's work.

Focus on what is possible rather than what is impossible — this is the first area for you to refocus.

Only you can determine your path

If your work life is empty, it's time now to ponder new possibilities. If you don't, who will?

First, you must start to believe that something you want is possible. Answer these questions for yourself:

With regard to my life's work, this is possible for me: _____.

I know this is possible because: _____.

If you are stuck on these two basic questions, you are not alone. Many people find it easier to focus on what's impossible. Those who focus on the impossible seldom change.

One thought leads to another

As you mull over new possibilities for your life, you will start to create new ideas you might not have considered before. Most of us start with what's impossible and then we stop.

Dinah, Justin, and Julie all took action after focusing on new possibilities. Soon, new and supportive beliefs followed.

Today, Dinah has released her first music CD, and Julie and Justin have founded Soccer Kids USA, a sports camp for children under age five.

How about you?

Only you can answer this question: "What is possible with my life's work?" for yourself. Here's how to get started:

- Define what's possible.
- Define new beliefs to support your new path.
- Write down the worst thing that could happen if you tried and failed.
- Write down the best thing that could happen if you succeeded.
- Decide who would be a good, supportive person to have along for the journey, and start spending more time with him or her.
- Decide who would not be as supportive, and start spending less time with them.
- Figure out who you can talk to — someone who is already doing what you want to do with your life's work.

Ask yourself new questions

What would your perfect life's work be?
In mid-life, it's a question we seldom ask. It could be the one question that saves you from lackluster jobs, faceless bosses, and endless commutes.

Are you stuck out of fear?
This happens to many people over forty. We get stuck in habit, routines, and day to day living.

What are you afraid of?

You probably fear the things most of us fear: damage to our relationships, our financial status, our routines, and our emotional state. After all, change is scary.

Don't wait for a mid-life crisis, make one
That's right; don't wait until you are forced to change by divorce, illness, job layoff, or financial disaster. That's what most people do.

Make your own mid-life crisis a crusade. This is what I did, and you can do it, too.

After twenty-five years in corporate America being good at what I did, but never liking it, I walked away. I walked away from faceless products, faceless bosses, and pointless meetings.

Since then, I have pursued my life's passion — helping others my age find the will and the strength to pursue their own passions.

This change has given me peace and joy because I am now living my life with authenticity and integrity. I am now being true to who I really am, but this change did not come without a price.

I had to give up my million-dollar house, and I ended up in bankruptcy. The best I could afford was a 400 square foot, one-bedroom apartment.

Living an authentic life also meant that I could no longer stay in my lifeless and abusive marriage. I dreamed about and then took action to find a new life partner who could support and believe in my authentic path.

As you can imagine, this was a very difficult time and there were days I wasn't sure that I would be able to feed my kids. One memory that will never leave me is trying to find a pawn shop to sell my wedding ring to buy food.

But my children and I grew closer as a family, and we had many fun-filled pizza and popcorn nights at home on the floor (no furniture!).

Although I didn't plan for this extreme situation, I did want to teach my kids a lesson about life and authenticity and what it means to live with integrity.

Will you go homeless or die?

You probably won't die but you may have to re-define what homeless means. Following your vocational passion is not easy. It may be the hardest thing you will ever do.

I had days with no money, no gas, and little food for the kids to eat. Yet somehow I always managed to come through when it counted.

Even as I went through this time of crisis, I wrote and published a book, started a private practice, and started teaching, speaking, and creating CDs and other products all targeted at those over forty.

My father's suicide not long after his retirement just served to strengthen my belief that we all should be doing what we love. If he had found and pursued his life's passion, perhaps he would still be alive today.

One of the things that got me through was my deep belief in my new life mission: that the world would be a better place if we all did what we love.

My survival secrets

Consider these secrets as you create your own path towards greater fulfillment and meaning in your life and work.

- Defeat your fears with actions that move you toward doing more of what you love.
- Seek out a support network of people who will honor your integrity and who will believe in you.
- Take a stand about something you believe in.
- Create your own work around your passions.
- Don't let the opinions of others get in the way.
- Get creative about how to make a living doing what you love.
- Downscale where possible to make the journey smoother.
- Do something small in your passions each day.
- Live with the intention that you will create work for yourself that is both fulfilling and meaningful.
- Smile a lot, laugh a lot, and be grateful for the life you have now.

As I continue to happily anticipate my work every day, I know I made the right choice. I feel positive and happy and I know that, although I may never be wealthy again, I will be able to build my business to the point where I can comfortably support myself and my family.

Best of all, I am now living with integrity — what a wonderful thing to be modeling for my kids!

Your life and work will be deeper and richer

Your life will be deeper because you will spend your days doing what you love. And richer because you have seen the *other* side, and in the process you have redefined for yourself what it means to live as a person with integrity.

Can you live an authentic life after 40?

You can live an authentic life after forty.

It will take hard work and it will take time. You will have to believe in yourself and your vision even when it seems that no one around you ever will. You will have to start looking at new possibilities for your life and your work.

But once you get going, the momentum will build and your life will never be the same. It's your time now to finally re-create your own life and your work.

Corporate manager turns to video production

Hank Bochenski, small business owner (ah, that's music to his ears) in San Ramon, California. For many years, Hank wanted to own his own business. Instead, he spent thirty years in the high technology industry working for large corporations in the data storage industry. His position there as a Customer Service Field Manager was very high pressure, and demanding, and Hank often ended the day feeling like the life blood had been drained out of him.

He often wondered: "How could I change my career now, after all these years, and do something I would enjoy."

He often heard the saying, "Find something you have a passion for, and do it for a living." Then Hank would ponder what his *possibilities* were.

He wondered how he could make a change and still maintain the lifestyle that he had become accustomed to.

In his spare time (there wasn't much because of his demanding career), Hank was converting his movie collection (over one thousand movies) from VHS to DVD. After converting the movies to DVD, and making DVD labels for each one of them, his wife said to him, "You know, it's too bad you can't make money doing that — it's the only time I see you happy."

That comment provided a moment of clarity for Hank, and a turning point in his life.

He did some research and found a company called Home Video Studio, Inc. located in Indianapolis. They offer a turnkey operation that provides a full range of support to new business owners interested in the video business. Their business package is amazing — the system, the equipment, the training, the support, the marketing materials, and so on.

What a perfect opportunity for someone like Hank. Hank and his wife did some due diligence and decided that this was a perfect opportunity for them. And to put the icing on the cake, Hank's studio is in his own home, and he no longer has to commute for hours every day.

Hank has been in business for several years now.

He says his life has never been so rewarding and fulfilling before, as he loves being a small business owner of Bochenski Video Services.

Occupational therapist answers the call

In 1999, Jennifer Wright took her first steps toward becoming a mid-life heroine, when, at age forty-seven, she moved halfway around the world. She grew up in the mid-west. She was a single parent of two children, and she worked as an occupational therapist (O.T.) in various clinical, educational, and management roles.

When her children left home, she felt the call to adventure.

Jennifer completed coaching training in 2003. Her O.T. experience in wellness, aging, and adventure therapy gave her a theoretical model on which to hang her coach's training. More of her future adventure plans came together on a backpacking trip to Nevada with her twenty-one year-old son, and she made her life-changing decision to move to New Zealand. She started to look at new *possibilities*. She systematically disordered her predictable life in order to re-create a new life in New Zealand.

An idea for an adventure coaching program for women in their mid-life transition led her to the creation of Mid-Life Adventure.

In addition to leading real-life six day/five night adventures in New Zealand, Jennifer offers life-changing coaching via teleclasses and one-to-one telephone coaching sessions. Most recently she released a ten-hour CD set with a workbook. Women use the CD to, in their own time, experience the life-changing power of "becoming a heroine," or the author of their own story at mid-life.

Women who are drawn to her program are between the ages of forty-five to sixty-five. They are looking for "more," and want a grounded, reality-based program.

Common issues are an empty nest, relationship challenges, lack of meaning in work and personal life, dealing with menopause in the workplace, dealing with chronic illness, and balancing career, aging parents, and a life for themselves.

Jennifer's long experience as an occupational therapist allows her to meet women "where they are" and provide just the right challenge. Jennifer's clients are able to quickly move from being frustrated, overwhelmed, and confused, to feeling empowered and finding meaning at mid-life.

Jennifer was featured in a May 15, 2005 cover story "Female Mid-Life Crisis: Bring It On" and most recently in a 60 Minutes documentary about her adventures in New Zealand.

Lessons to learn

Sometimes it takes rocking the boat and changing your life completely to answer the call for a more authentic life.

When you start to believe that something is indeed possible for you in your vocational life, and you have the courage to follow your heart, magical things can happen. This takes courage and you must take a risk. There is a difference between just deciding to change your life and taking the action required to make the change. It takes a complete shift in thought, and in many cases, it involves over-turning the apple cart of your life. This is radical change, and not one most people are accustomed to. This is, however, just the right recipe for those over forty whose lives have become both predictable and secure.

After the forty milestone, we need to put aside our egos. The ego is useful before age forty, but after forty, we need to replace ego with cause and integrity.

Life has a way of moving much faster in mid-life. This is not the time for pondering or worrying or over-analyzing. This is the time for action. Not just mindless action, but action that will lead to more joy, more happiness, and more meaning in your life.

This approach isn't just for the most secure or the most fortunate; it is for everyone wishing to create a better life. Wonderful things can happen when your life is centered around your true vocation. Your work can determine who you are and who you become. Just think back to work you did in the past and how quickly it became the norm for you — you felt like this job was your life. This is how quickly our work can consume us.

If you don't pay attention to your growing angst, your life can pass too quickly, and suddenly you find yourself talking about your past and what might have been. Thinking deeply now about new possibilities instead will fill your mind with new creativity, new energy, and the expectation of a fuller life centered around your work and passions. This great opportunity awaits everyone after forty. The ticket is yours to use or discard along the road to *someday*.

Your new possibilities await you now. All you have to do is take action.

Place

What is your role in the world?

In your heart, what is the vision you have for yourself? What are your abilities and your interests? Do they match?

Having an internal vision of your place (role) in the world is an important recognition. Some roles will just seem to fit you more naturally than others.

When you were a small child, what did you want to do when you grew up? Now as an adult, what do you want to do when you grow up?

Start to ponder deeply the role you want to play and why. Approach this exercise diligently, and your life will never be the same.

Why people ignore their inner needs at mid-life

It seems to me that many people tend to ignore their needs in mid-life. We tend to be very good at reacting to a crisis, but terrible at planning for one.

And the middle of a crisis is the worst time to consider our place in the world with regards to our work. I think this is the root of the problem. For example, many people stay in mundane, unfulfilling jobs because, in many ways, this is easier than confronting the unhappiness of an empty work life. Only when a crisis hits, and it usually will after forty — a divorce, a layoff, an illness, children going off to college, money problems, or emotional problems — do people finally spring into action.

Why does it take so long to decide to change?

While many people over forty no longer feel contented with their work, they may still be just challenged enough that they are not driven to make a change. As a result, their moods and their responses to their work tend to go up and down depending on the day. They may be very negative one day, but then the next day is a little better, and they postpone making a change yet again.

It also can be easy to escape the need to change — people become so busy each and every day that busyness itself becomes the escape and the excuse.

Beware of the simple tasks

Some will suggest that mundane jobs are good. Mundane and boring work gives you time to think about other things, perhaps even allowing time to work on other things.

People feel trapped by the promise of reward and the threat of punishment at work. This too becomes a trap that's difficult to escape from.

There is a lever in the cage of work

Early experiments by B. F. Skinner involved placing animals in a cage without an escape route. Then later, he added a lever that operated a door inside the cage, and eventually the animals figured out how to leave the cage.

For humans, the escape lever is there all the time, but it takes a crisis for us to be able to see it. It is much too easy to become trapped by what is comfortable and routine until we suddenly find the secret to escaping.

Our self-worth gets damaged when we have JUST a job

When we experience any failure in life, and especially in our work, we hesitate before trying anything new again because failing again will hurt even more.

People over forty who have built their lives in this way are very risk-averse. Any new venture or idea must be checked with others for approval. If our peers do not approve, then surely we must not take a chance.

Discussing with co-workers that you are no longer finding joy in your work doesn't help; this subject causes more discomfort than discussing sex. They don't know how to respond. There doesn't seem to be an immediate solution. After all, work is work, isn't it?

The problem: WE live our lives

You are the person who has to live with yourself. You have to look at yourself in the mirror each day, go to work, be active, and be comfortable with your decisions.

Regardless of what others think or see in you, it is your own perspective of you that matters most.

Your work determines who you are

I see so many clients who initially come with their arms crossed. I see right away that it is not *their* arms that are crossed, but perhaps their parents' arms, or their spouses' arms. All of us carry a huge set of beliefs passed down to us from others.

To prove the point, take a piece of paper right now, and write down the following:

"I believe the following about myself:"

Now list those things you believe are true about yourself.

When you have finished, examine your list. How many of these beliefs have come from you, and how many came from those around you?

Now go through your list and change those beliefs that are no longer useful. For example, perhaps you wrote on your list that you were practical, and didn't take unnecessary risks. Now you realize that your parents taught you never to take a risk, or try anything silly, or impractical. Reflect how this has kept you from changing your work — is it really fear of failure?

Change those beliefs on your list that are no longer useful. It is as simple, and as difficult as this. I believe change can occur in seconds. It's all a matter of acquiring a new perspective about your life and your work.

It's time to re-create

If you are a mid-life adult who no longer finds meaning and joy in your work, you must make a change now. The changes you make now will impact the rest of your life. If you don't, you will simply work until you retire, spend a few years wondering what you *could* have done, and then, well — you know the rest of the story...

Traditional approaches to career development do not work

Traditional career coaching focuses on assessments to figure out exactly what you should do.

The problem with this approach is that, while these systematic methods may recommend that you should be an engineer, for example, only you can determine whether you would actually find joy and passion in this work.

Most traditional job searches are done backwards. A job gets posted and people look to see if the job matches some of their requirements.

The problem with this approach is that these jobs were not designed with you in mind. They were not designed around what — exactly — would be just perfect for you.

Don't ignore your inner needs after 40

The most important questions to ask after age forty are:

Is my work meaningful? Is the purpose of my work obvious to me? Is it clear why I am doing this work? Does my work bring me joy and happiness?

You must answer these questions for yourself.

Make an honest assessment of what you want

Self-discovery and work renewal will result in more passion and joy in your life and in the lives of all those around you.

You will wonder why you didn't start earlier.

Maybe you didn't take the plunge earlier because you did not experience the crisis until right now — that is, the crisis of your mid-life — and now you plan to make the second half of your life even better.

This can start with your work. You have the wisdom and maturity now to make this change.

Remember: The only permission you need is permission from yourself.

Does finding my place in the world require change?

Do I have to change who I am to do what I love?

The answer is yes. When you go from one lackluster job to another one, not much personal change is needed.

But when you go from "just a job" to a vocation — that is, doing what you love — it does require a change. It requires a coming-out party, of sorts. It requires a "lifting the cover" off your true, authentic self. It requires risk-taking, creativity, and a new way of thinking about your work and life.

Meet Carl and Monica

Carl Battiste was a sales executive doing all the right things — all the things society has taught us to do. Carl worked hard to support his family. He had a growing feeling of being trapped, even though his job brought in plenty of money. One day, Carl just couldn't take it anymore. He realized that the pain of not changing was suddenly greater than the pain involved with changing. Carl was passionate about real estate, so he made the leap. The real estate market has been very tough, but he has never been happier.

Monica Lee, a grandmother of ten, now just shy of sixty years old and an artist, remembers back when she made the big change. Shortly after turning forty, she realized that her passion was painting. Despite the uncertainty of making ends meet each month, and initially having to live in the back of her gallery while she rented out her house, and despite the makeshift bed, and showers with a garden hose, she knew this was what she had to do.

It is not easy to make big changes like this, and it may take great sacrifice. It will require emotional strength, an unshakable belief in yourself, and a willingness to take risks with your life.

How you can apply these lessons for yourself?

First, decide what you really want to do. Figure out what you are good at, and what you really enjoy. This is where you should focus.

All the rules we learn in school and through life about improving our weaknesses, are a waste of time and life. If you do this, you will be able to do lots of things, but they will all lack energy and passion. It is much better to focus your life's work and all your efforts on what you really love to do.

What's the worst that could happen if you do change?

Asking yourself this question is a healthy exercise. I doubt that you will die, or even go homeless.

I have discovered that when people do what they love, they suddenly find new creativity they didn't know they had, and they figure out new ways to make the money they need to keep doing what they love.

This is almost like an addiction, but this addiction is good for your soul!

What's the best that could happen if you do change?

This is an even better question to ask. Think about how the relationships in your life will improve. Think about how much happier you will be. Think about how much more energy you will have in your life.

How do you achieve what you want?

First envision what you want. Write down exactly what you want to do.

Start talking to others now about this dream. Each day, take small steps toward your dream. These steps might be research, reading, taking a class, or talking to someone else who already does what you want to do.

Measure your progress as you go. It is true that what gets measured, gets done — it forces you to reflect on your progress.

Finally, reward yourself every step of the way. Small rewards you give yourself can be the best gifts of all.

What is at stake if you don't change?

This is the most important question of all. If you cannot answer this question, you will not take any action. If you cannot define for yourself what the effect of not changing will have on your life, you will not change. Only when you clearly see the result of not changing, will you suddenly find the inner strength to change.

Remaining who you are is not sufficient

To live with vocational passion and do work that can last a lifetime takes courage, action, and creativity. It will also take a coming-out party for the real you — the you who is no longer worried about what others will think.

Change is hard, but only through difficult change will you really grow and, as a result, gain new perspectives about yourself and your world.

Engineer turned author helps others

Anita Flegg spent eighteen years as an electrical engineer. She enjoyed it for the first half of that time, but it stopped being satisfying after a while. After all the time and effort in getting the engineering degree, Anita felt that she really had to stick with it. Besides, the pay was really good, so it was hard to imagine quitting, even if she knew what she wanted to do instead. In the last couple of years it took all her energy just to keep going.

As Anita approached her fortieth birthday, she realized she just couldn't keep this up. She knew all along there was more she could be doing with her life. She made a plan to retire from engineering work by age forty, but despite all the various aptitude tests she had taken over the years, she still didn't know what she would do next.

Then it happened — at age thirty-nine and a half, Anita was laid off. After the initial shock, she felt released and free. She decided to use her new free time to spend time with family and get in shape. She was overweight and always tired. She started working out twice a week, and walking every day, but still she was not losing weight. She also continued to have a strange group of physical symptoms. With a little research, she discovered she had hypoglycemia.

She turned to research, and as she started to cure herself, she discovered a new cause; helping others through writing. She wrote her first book on hypoglycemia and knew that this was what she was meant to do. This was her *place* in the world — to write — and there was no turning back from her perfect vocational day.

Anita first published *Hypoglycemia: The Other Sugar Disease* in 2003, and she has now released the second edition of the book and started a business, The Sharp Quill, so that she can write and edit full time.

From mid-life to pet-sitting in Dublin, Ireland

The idea had been niggling at Claire Hegarty for years, but only when she got a bit of a fright did she take any action. For years she didn't have the courage, confidence, or motivation to do anything about it.

Claire had a job that was comfortable, and close to home, and she was well-paid — why bother to change anything?

Then Claire read about someone who had taken ill suddenly, at the age of forty-one, and in the middle of a stressful presentation had dropped dead. She realized she was hurtling towards forty, and if she wasn't careful she would be going into the next bit of her life doing exactly what she was doing now. She might even keel over before she got to take action on her idea.

Claire had always spent a lot of her time doing things for other people, but she started thinking about what else she could do in life.

First on the list: family and friends. As these were things she spent time on anyway, she felt that area was fine. Next on the list: her love of animals, specifically dogs and cats. And third: her love of writing and technology.

There she had it! Why not combine all of the things she loved? Claire realized that her *place* in the world was becoming clear.

The first thing she did was take an animal care course in the evenings at the local college.

Then she started putting up ads for a dog walking and pet-sitting service everywhere she could think of. At the local veterinary surgeons, on notice boards at shops and supermarkets, and by telling everyone she met.

Next, Claire bought a cheap, do-it-yourself web editor and learned some website programming from the Internet. She was amazed at the amount of free information to be gleaned from the Internet. She learned everything she needed to know about marketing, advertising, and creating a website. She got in touch with other pet-sitters, specifically in the US and the UK, as it is a relatively new industry in Ireland.

Within months Claire had registered the business, set it up, and acquired a decent client base with regular customers. She could not imagine why she had not done this earlier!

Now Claire finds the business is gaining momentum. She does all the morning, evening, and weekend work and her helper takes care of the business on weekdays. She is still in her daytime job, but she is working steadily at her own business with a view to running it full-time in the very near future.

Claire is so much happier and healthier, and a lot more confident. There is just no compensation greater than doing what you love.

Lessons to learn

Anita and Claire both listened to their inner signals that something wasn't quite right in their work life, and took action to improve the happiness and quality of their vocational life.

Changes like this don't happen overnight. It takes hard work; you must think deeply about your place in the world. We aren't taught this in life. Unless we were fortunate enough to have a parent who encouraged us to follow our heart, or we had a great mentor along the way, most adults fall into a job early in their life, and never escape from job prison.

In today's economy, with so many people being laid off, this is the free ticket to a more authentic life. Being dismissed from a job feels shocking, humiliating, and very scary indeed. For most people, though, the job that was lost was simply a means to pay the rent, and that's all. This can be the perfect time to reevaluate your life and place in the world.

For both Anita and Claire, it took external events to drive them to change. It was only through an internal shift that they were able to think for themselves about what really mattered and how they could pursue it.

Finding your place in the world takes a review of your life and in some ways, a reconciliation of what has occurred.

Rather than viewing the past as time wasted, perform this life review in a positive way. Realize that what you did in the past was necessary at the time, and in fact led to exactly where you should be right now. The present is all we have to make changes.

Many people spend their days feeling badly about the past and worried about the future. A better strategy is to take action now — in the present. This takes deep reflection followed by action. Most people know deep inside the work that feels like the best fit, but they provide reasons and justification to explain why pursuing these dreams are silly, not practical or real. As a result, many people never do work that feels authentic.

The motivation and insight you need to find your place in the world must come from within you. It also takes some trial and error. Like Anita's and Claire's stories show, it takes action to make your dreams a reality.

Position

What is your attitude on a daily basis?

What would you like to change about your attitude toward your work? Why? What small steps could you take now to try on a new daily position?

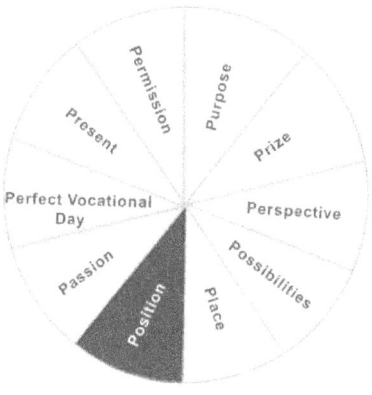

Your daily position — your attitude — is critical. It either drives you forward to your goals or keeps you away from what you want most in life.

Most of us have negative attitudes when it comes to our work. I have news for you — work doesn't have to be something you do only for a paycheck, and that you don't need to love, or even like. Your work can be joyful and full of meaning. You can feel great about it.

The secret, of course, is taking the right steps to discover what you most love to do. The result? You will have work that will last a lifetime, and that you will always be proud of and feel great about. What a gift you will give yourself and others with your new position — attitude — about your life and your work.

What is your attitude towards your work?

The position you take just might mean the difference between fulfillment and misery.

On a recent trip to teach and speak in Russia, I discovered that our culture can influence our position or attitude about our work.

In Russia, for example, the pairing of work and joy doesn't compute. The general feeling in Russia is that one's work is something that must be done whether one likes it or not.

In North America, while there is a growing trend to choose our work more carefully, there still are remarkably similar attitudes about work.

Mid-life is the chance to readjust your position

Mid-life is the perfect time to change or even re-create your attitude about your work.

It's time to discard ideas that are no longer useful, and replace them with more useful ideas.

This is not easy

Now, almost eight years removed from corporate America, I have had many days and nights wondering, "What am I doing?!"

Trading a six-figure income managing other people in their jobs for days spent writing books like this? Trying to give people new ideas how to discover and do what they love? Spending hour after hour in my private practice discussing with clients the same fears, and concerns I experienced?

In spite of this, I feel eager anticipation every day helping people as they re-create their work lives.

"This isn't a real job," I often think. "What am I doing while all those *other* people commute to their real jobs?"

Work and joy do fit together

Having an attitude about your work that you must not only enjoy, but love what you do is not just reserved for the privileged in our society.

Sure, it may be harder for some people to get started, but just because we all have different starting lines doesn't mean we can't all join the race to an authentic work life.

Are you too comfortable in your job?

Up to age forty or so, many of us have settled into a comfortable pattern of work. We don't necessarily love it, or even like it, but it pays the bills and helps build our egos.

You can live a more authentic life by starting to change your position about your work.

Mid-life is a time of attitude adjustment

Is what you do *just* a job to retire from? Or do you want to do activities each and every day that you love, and that you never have to stop doing until you die?

The only people who retire are people who don't love what they do. Are you one of them?

You can live a more authentic life, but the changes must come from you. If you don't change your position and the direction of your work, then who will?

I am still waiting for the first Human Resources benefits package that offers "Authentic life" with the 401K program and two weeks vacation, but I am not holding my breath!

Will this be hard work?

Changing your position or attitude about your work may be the hardest thing you have ever done. You will have to defeat external attitudes about work. These attitudes will come from co-workers, bosses, spouses, and mothers-in-law.

Second, you may need to build the self-confidence you'll need to stand up for your new attitude.

It all starts with you

Can you think of someone you know who has a great attitude about his or her work? How can you try on a similar attitude about your work?

Our beliefs about work may have to go. Many of us have beliefs that don't fit us any longer, but we hold on to them like an old familiar coat. Sometimes we forget it's our life we are living, not our father's or our mother's or our wife's or our husband's.

What can you do now? Ten steps to get started NOW

1. Expect to find happiness in your work and be prepared to search for it.

2. Get rid of old patterns of thoughts and attitudes that are no longer useful for your work.
3. Don't expect anyone else to change your attitude for you.
4. Do expect lots of resistance from others.
5. Practice your new attitude about your work every day.
6. Discard all negative thoughts about your work as quickly as possible. Instead, change your work.
7. Take a new position that you will no longer settle for unfulfilling work that has no meaning in your life.
8. Create an inner awareness that the second half of your life can be authentic, happier, and more satisfying.
9. Smile and laugh more in mid-life. You can defeat negativity this way.
10. Expect to discover and do what you love.
11. Practice a consistent daily attitude that is the same in the morning and at night. This will help you feel calmer about yourself and your work.

More fruit on your cereal

Now that you are over forty, you may have adopted a new diet, and a new exercise schedule. Maybe your relationships are improving, and you might even be sleeping better. What can possibly be better than this?

Well, creating a new attitude or position about your work is like adding fruit on your cereal in the morning. It will put a smile on your face and a bounce in your step.

In mid-life, this might just be what we need the most. When you decide to change your position or attitude about what you want in your life, momentum and energy builds and change becomes possible.

Kevin — beyond "the Wall"

After more than twenty years of just making a living to provide for his family, Kevin O'Neil hit the wall, or more literally, the carpet.

On the day before Kevin was to start a new sales job, he was hanging drapery in his family's living room. A leg on the ladder buckled, and he was thrown to the ground. Kevin started the job with a bruised shoulder, but a couple of visits to the doctor, and an X-ray showed he had broken his humerus and torn his rotator cuff. He was just starting his new job, and now he needed surgery and he had to take time off to recover — several weeks of recuperation and months of physical therapy to get his range of motion back.

Kevin really didn't have a choice. It was either leave his new job — before it even got off the ground — or risk never regaining full use of his left arm.

With his left arm immobile, and pain medications keeping him from working effectively, Kevin was forced to confront what he wanted to do with the rest of his life. Kevin decided a shift in his position or attitude, and the way he thought about his work, was required.

Two decades earlier, on the same day Kevin received his Masters degree in Industrial Organizational Psychology, his wife found out she was pregnant with their first child. Rather than taking that first low paying internship job in Organizational Development, Training or HR, Kevin abandoned his dream, choosing instead to pursue a sales career — something he thought would pay better.

He learned the hard way — through recessions, company restructuring, outsourcing, and downsizing — that even in good times, working just to survive doesn't cut it in the long run.

After Kevin's shoulder started to feel better, he temporarily went back to sales, writing advertising copy for an online auction house, and trying to become quiet enough to figure out his true role in the world. After a few months of rehabilitation and word processing, Kevin knew he wanted to start something new — but what?

What was he really passionate about?

Kevin decided to revisit his graduate school interests, and poked around the organizational development field. Jobs were still scarce, and his experience had taught him that corporate life had become meaner and colder over time. He had to ask himself, "Do I still think there is a chance for me to help make the work life of employees within a company more humane?"

Kevin's perceptions of today's corporations were by now 180 degrees opposite of what they had been, and he didn't think he could wholeheartedly facilitate organizational changes.

Kevin made a deep and clear-headed self-assessment. What could he do? What did he really want to do?

Peeling back the years, Kevin remembered wanting to be a counselor, but he didn't think he had the time or resources to get another advanced degree. He was volunteering as a mediator in Small Claims Court, but not being an attorney, he learned that creating a paying job as mediator in his region is a long process, requiring an intense amount of networking to find even an occasional assignment.

Kevin wondered, "How can I recombine my skills and experiences into a new career?"

Kevin and his wife have raised an autistic son, now seventeen years old, and they went through all the changes one might expect for a special-needs family. Their journey was so important to Kevin's wife, Sharon, that she was inspired to build on her teaching career. She earned a Special Education Credential, becoming a Certified Behavioral Intervention Case Manager (BICM).

Building on his wife's skills and his own, Kevin launched The O'Neil Advocacy Group, a professional consultancy dedicated to helping families with special needs children. Kevin and his wife help facilitate the development of action plans to get the services families with special needs children require.

Stressful situations occur every day when a family is living with a special needs child. Kevin and Sharon coach positive, effective behavioral management strategies that aid and enrich the daily lives of every member of the family.

So far, Kevin and Sharon have launched a website, built a referral network of more than fifty professionals and parents, designed a brochure, and scheduled speaking engagements. They are now writing a current and comprehensive directory of services in two counties in their area. Just by contacting their son's Regional Center Case Manager, Kevin and Sharon's business is now linked to eight different Regional Center Case Management work teams.

Kevin is now feeling very positive; and he has every reason to believe that by continuing their outreach, The O'Neil Advocacy Group will soon be a very busy and successful practice. His position about his work has changed and so has his life's work.

Lessons to learn

It takes a shift in your thinking to make vocational change. It is easy to accept an ongoing negative position about your life when you are handed what seems like a losing deck of cards. But like the losing gambler who has to learn when to stop, it takes walking away from the table and starting a new game. This new game needs to include new rules that you create. These new rules must come from within you. They must align to what is most important in your life and work.

For Kevin, it would have been easy to simply give up on his dreams, surviving doing what they already knew how to do despite having a negative attitude about their work.

Instead Kevin somehow found the courage to make change from the inside out. As a result, his position about his work — and who he is — changed for good.

It is easy to blame others for our mishaps. After forty, especially, this is not useful. In mid-life we must become a little selfish and pursue a second half of life that brings more joy, more meaning, and work that can enable us to smile each and every day.

Misery seems to love company and many people seem to find comfort by surrounding themselves with others who are negative about their life and their work.

The good news is that as long we are breathing we have the opportunity to improve our outlook and attitude — our position — about our life and our work. Again this is difficult work because it must be done alone, and without consulting others. The returns will be great, including a lifelong feeling of inner peace, satisfaction, and deep happiness. Following your heart and changing your attitude or position about your work will change your life forever.

Passion

How can I find it and keep it?

What are you really passionate about? Can you identify the vocational patterns (areas where you could earn a living) in your passions?

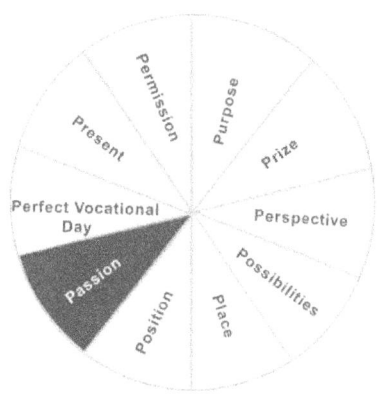

From Merriam-Webster dictionary, *passion* (applicable to vocation) is defined as:

> ***4a:*** *the emotions as distinguished from reason,* ***b:*** *intense, driving, or overmastering feeling or conviction*
>
> ***5a****: ardent affection:* LOVE, ***b:*** *a strong liking or desire for or devotion to some activity, object, or concept,* ***d:*** *an object of desire or deep interest*

Passion is enthusiasm applied to an activity that is lively and exciting. Passion is about an energetic and unflagging pursuit, aim or devotion to a cause that is important to you.

It is important to identify your passion, and once you have identified it, you must find your vocational patterns.

Getting up each morning with sincere excitement about doing work that is focused on your passions will bring new meaning to your life, who you are, and why you do what you do.

Don't let negativity defeat creativity!

How do you discover and live your passion?

This is a question we all want to answer, especially in mid-life where everything is suddenly up for questioning. Especially after age forty, when you get this nagging feeling that what you do isn't really fulfilling and meaningful anymore, and when your support structure continues to be more concerned with the mundane aspects of life than with happiness and fulfillment.

How do you discover your passion in your work?

Another tough question.

For me, it was in the middle of teaching a workshop years ago while I was still working in corporate America. I had a sudden awareness that my life had to change. It was in the middle of yet another slide presentation. I felt dizzy, and light-headed. My boss thought perhaps I was getting sick, and said we should reschedule.

I remember thinking to myself; *I was sick all right — sick of this job.* What I really needed to do was reschedule my life.

You can start by writing down what gets you the most excited about life. Is it riding your bike on Sunday mornings, spending time alone with your books, or doing the budget back at the office on Thursday afternoons? The answer is different for each of us.

Think deeply about it and write down what excites you most.

Imagine

Imagine what your life would be like if you spent the majority of your day actually doing what you love — what a concept!

Many people are unable to do this because they immediately jump to the conclusion that they couldn't support themselves and their families doing what they love. Sadly, they wait until they retire. Then something happens and they die. Then it really *is* too late.

Hang around others who love what you love

The next best step is to meet and hang around people who love what you love. Discussing your passion with like-minded people will give you ideas.

If you love books, start attending book fairs and libraries; meet with publishers, authors, and editors and visit book stores. Meet and observe others who spend their days with books.

If you love to work with numbers, start meeting and hanging around with similar people. Subscribe to financial publications, talk to accountants, controllers, and other people who work with money and spreadsheets all day. Learn what they do, how they do it, and why they do it.

This will give you new ideas.

Build a life roadmap

Determine what is most important to you in your life. Figure out what you need to do each and every day to align your actions with what is most important to you. Establish key goals for the next three to five years that align with what is most important to you. Make sure your goals align with your passions.

What is vocational passion?

Imagine it's Sunday night and you can't get to sleep. You toss and turn all night thinking about your work. You wake up and glance at the clock. It's still only two o'clock, and then it's four o'clock, and then finally it's five o'clock. You can't stand it anymore. You jump out of bed thinking about all the work you must accomplish on Monday.

The difference is this: when your work is also your vocational passion, your lack of sleep will be like a child's Christmas Eve excitement, and you'll love every minute of it.

Your work takes your breath away

I gave a talk to a large group recently about how to discover and follow your passion. As I was waiting off-stage listening to the MC introduce me, my usual pre-talk feelings overwhelmed me. I felt dizzy, and a little light-headed, and my body felt a rush of breath.

Although I am in great shape for my age, I worried that I was having a stroke, and that I would die shortly into my talk. Then I thought to myself, *I hope it doesn't happen until the end of my talk, or at least the funny parts.*

My thoughts were interrupted as I heard, "And here is Craig Nathanson, The Vocational Coach." Within seconds, thoughts of an impending heart attack or stroke left me, and as I saw my audience, I suddenly, once again, felt my purpose in the world.

This inner experience happens every time I speak, and just before meeting with my clients. I have come to realize that this is the rush of vocational passion. Each time, I am convinced once again that I have found a way to continue living an authentic life doing what I love.

Do you toss and turn on Sunday night?

Do you jump out of bed on Monday morning and race to work? Is Monday your best day of the week, and is Friday the worst because you have to wait until the following Monday to resume your life's work?

Believe it or not, this really *is* possible!

How do you live your vocational passion?

It sounds simple and yet this is the most challenging thing: take action.

In spite of all the people who tell you you're crazy; you'll starve; you're selfish; you'll be homeless; *you do it anyway*. You start to take action with the intention of figuring out a way to make this work.

Even if you start at Harry's Hoff Brau

After leaving a senior management position in corporate America over eight years ago, it was always an interesting experience telling people what I did. To the usual party question, "So what do you do?" I would simply say, "I work with people over forty to help them discover and do what they love!"

The look in their eyes always said something between, "You fool!" and "I am jealous!"

My first talk was scheduled to be in front of a big crowd as part of a job fair at Harry's Hoff Brau in San Jose, California. As I entered the room about five minutes before my talk, I wondered if I was in the wrong room — it was empty. Around six p.m. when my talk was about to start, a sweet elderly woman in her late eighties wandered in and asked if the show was about to begin. She was recently widowed after fifty years of marriage and she was carrying around a lot of sadness. She thought this free show might cheer her up.

I sat down next to her, and just listened to her talk about her life.

Although I didn't give my planned speech, when she hugged me and told me I had cheered her up, I thought to myself that it had been a perfect first show.

What matters most is that you START

Following your vocational passion, especially after forty, is a lonely experience at first. Soon, however, you will become so involved in doing what you love that you will start to wonder why it took you so long to get started.

I remember picking up my then seven year-old son from school one day. As I waited for him, a woman drove up and asked, "Are you the guy I read about in the paper recently who helps people discover and do what they love?" I said, "Well, yes I am."

She said, "I noticed you the other day before the article came up and I thought to myself, *There is a man with bounce in his step.*"

I picked up my son and as we drove away, I thought to myself, "That's what happens when you live an authentic life — you get that bounce in your step!"

Can you get the bounce back in your step?

I think you can. First imagine what you want and what you are passionate about.

Make your passions work for you

Making your passions work for you is important because your happiness matters and makes a difference in your life.

Imagine waking up day after day to the work you love to do. Believe it or not, this can be your real life.

After we turn forty, things change. If we admit it to ourselves, deep inside we wish we could do more with our lives. Our concerns usually center around our work.

At this stage of life, we tend to give up our dreams and settle on doing just a job, hoping to retire one day so we can finally do what we love to do.

But will that day ever come?

Where do you stand?

Do you know what you are passionate about? Are you working at something you are passionate about?

If you didn't answer yes to both questions, you have more to do. Many people over forty just assume it's too late. They feel society's pressure to slow down, conserve, and save money.

Are you saving too much?

Recent research by a small group research institution suggests that Americans are currently saving too much. (CNN Money, April 2007)

The report suggests that we should get more out of our money while we are young. Otherwise, we risk losing opportunities to enjoy what we have because we are saving for when we're older.

Of course this advice would be frowned on by almost every financial firm — they have great ideas for using our money. Most of these firms suggest that the average person will need an annual retirement income equal to 75 to 86% of what he or she earned in their final year of employment.

When you do what you love and have a lighter backpack, you never need to retire

When I talk about traveling with a lighter backpack, I mean reducing expenses by eliminating those things we don't really need. We need to recognize that keeping up with the neighbors isn't making us happy, Think about it: will having a slightly larger TV make us happier? Will replacing our car with the latest model really make us happier? Do we need a home with more rooms than we use every day? We need to lighten our backpacks to accommodate those things and expenses that really make our lives work, while eliminating those things that only make us look good to others.

What the financial firms don't understand is that with a lighter backpack, we can, in fact, work forever doing what we love and earn the income we require. When we work in our vocation, there is no final year of employment until we stop breathing.

What happens if you wait too long?

If you wait too long, your quality of life decreases. Life feels mundane, and your goals no longer seem interesting. Your loved ones suddenly become your scapegoats. You start to feel sluggish and you end up spending too many hours on the couch watching mindless television.

On the other hand, making your passion work can make you a bit giddy.

The first steps

Evaluate what you want. This is always the easiest step, but also the most difficult. Figuring out what you want takes an honest self-assessment. Find out who else shares your passion and actually makes an income doing what you love. You'll be surprised what you discover. For example, let's say you love building model airplanes, but you need to make $75,000 a year to keep your family running smoothly. Not enough people to sell airplanes to? No problem.

You could:

- Start your own store and call it, "Model Planes for You."
- Work for a model plan manufacturer as a sales rep to get started.

- Start an Internet site as a place for model plane hobbyists to gather, and gather revenue from ads and other means.
- Start a business organizing model airplane parties for kids.
- Offer team building events to corporate America that involve building paper airplanes. Attendees would see which group's paper airplane flies the farthest. Corporate America loves to spend money on this kind of event.

You might have several income-producing activities, along with perhaps working a couple of days a week at a local hobby store to make ends meet in the short term.

Prepare to downscale

I have seldom seen a person make his passion work without some initial downscaling. This doesn't mean forever, just initially.

This might scare many baby boomers to run in the other direction — fast. After all, what would we do without our SUVs (and their lease payments), our large mortgages, and our retirement nest eggs?

Well, I guarantee we would be freer and lighter and better able to explore new possibilities for making our passions work.

Working hard — with a difference

There is a difference between working hard so that one day you can live your passions, and making your passion work for you right now.

Sales exec finds passion in a nonprofit

Jim Goebelbecker was just shy of forty years old. In February 2004, Jim was given notice that the company he'd joined three months earlier was going out of business. His third child was only two months old. And although he was enjoying the business development job, Jim's inner sense told him that high-pressure sales was not his forte.

But what would he do for work? Jim knew that he needed some objective help. In a safe and trusting environment where he was engaged in personal conversation, Jim was encouraged to dream, and to accept nothing less than a life of passion-filled activities.

Jim then found an ideal role. He's now the Director of Administration for a local nonprofit that provides family housing. And an additional bonus — his office is only ten minutes away from his home.

The job has been everything Jim was looking for. It provides an opportunity to practice the organizational development skills he'd been learning. He has direct impact on strategic planning and implementation. He provides custom training and leadership development. He's exposed to complex human resource issues. And, Jim has a flexible schedule so he can finish his doctorate program.

Jim's joy at work has positively influenced his relationship with his wife, too. She sees how happy he is with his new gig, and likes the contribution he's making to the growing organization. Jim's positive mental and emotional state have brought more lightness and fun into their relationship.

Jim continues to review the work he has done and he plans to revisit his yearly goals on a regular basis so that they become reality.

All Jim wants to do in his life now are the things he loves to do!

Writer Robin follows her passion

After a painful divorce, Robin Sparks decided it was now her time to follow her *passion* of writing and traveling. Despite the solo journey following her heart, Robin became clear about her life's purpose. It was to travel the world and tell the stories of others.

Despite the urging of friends and family not to change, Robin ignored both the advice and the status quo to follow her heart. She learned that to recover from past wounds in her life it was necessary to acknowledge them, and then start to move forward to write a new chapter of her life.

Today, Robin Sparks is a writer and photographer who teaches the art of storytelling in workshops around the world. Her love of writing, travel, and teaching make for dynamic, life-changing classes.

Robin's stories and photographs have since been published in hundreds of magazines, newspapers, newsletters, and online ezines.

Robin began her professional life telling stories as a newspaper photographer in Denver, Colorado in 1977.

Last year two of Robin's photos were chosen for inclusion in the photo coffee table books "Friends" and "Family" published by M.I.L.K.

Robin currently writes a monthly column for Metro Magazine in Bangkok, Thailand and the online magazine, EscapeArtist.com as well as occasional travel stories for the *San Francisco Chronicle*.

She is currently writing a book about her encounters with American expatriates around the world from

London, to Bangkok, from Katmandu to Brazil, and beyond.

Lessons to learn

Following your passion can be a lonely journey in the early stages. Persistence and the courage to live a life of integrity can make the journey possible, and more rewarding.

It takes time, energy, and a lot of patience to find your passion and place in the world. With a little persistence, though, this goal is possible for all of us.

Perhaps the most important thing we can learn from Jim's and Robin's experiences is to trust our internal and external signs. If something appears missing in your life, it's crucial to listen to yourself and then take decisive action. Nothing happens until you take action to change your life.

Many people spend more time evaluating the worst things that might happen when making positive vocational change. But what we focus on is often what we get more of; the more negative outcomes are pondered, the higher the likelihood these events will occur.

Instead, focus on the best that could happen. Thinking positively encourages more positive thinking to emerge.

Jim and Robin discovered that the more they believed in new possibilities and new outcomes, the more confident they felt. After that, there was no turning back.

Think deeply about what proof you will need to convince yourself it is possible to follow your heart and enjoy your work. With each small step, your self-confidence and your spirit and energy will increase. Like Jim and Robin, you will become clearer about your passions and how you can spend the rest of your life doing work you love.

Perfect Vocational Day

How to discover and experience it

Do you have a vision of your perfect day?

Would you go after it if you could live it while also making the income you require?

If you can't imagine it, you can't move towards it. Let's define the *Perfect Vocational Day:*

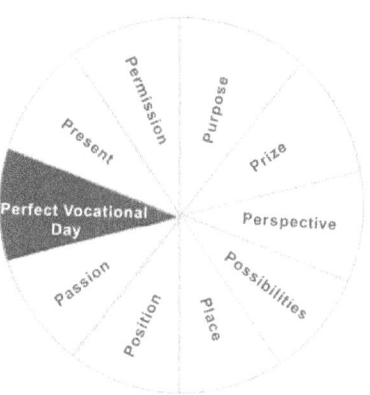

- You spend your day doing activities that you feel passionate about.
- These activities give you energy and a sense of purpose every day.
- Your perfect vocational day gives you a sense of fulfillment and gives your life meaning. Your activities feel like a good match of your abilities and your interests.
- Your work is maximally expressive of your passions, given existing constraints. Your work meets your existing personal needs.

If you can't dream it, you can't move towards it. It is important to use all your senses: sight, touch, smell, taste, and hearing.

You can be the artist for your life and your work, but first you must decide what you will paint. With this vision, you can create a masterpiece that will nourish you and provide a foundation for your entire life.

Envision and live your perfect vocational day

Have you ever thought about what your perfect work would be? Think about the pattern of a typical work day for the rest of your life. What daily routine would make you feel excited, and bring joy and happiness to your work?

How do I get started?

Whether you work for yourself or someone else, it is critical to start with the idea of what would be just perfect for you.

For example, when would you get up in the morning? Once up, what would your morning routine be? Would you start your day exercising, with a little run, or perhaps some yoga or meditation? Or would you make breakfast first instead? Would you eat alone or with others? If you are with others, who would they be?

What would you wear to your work?

Sweats, suit, shorts?

What would be just perfect for you?

I'm sure by now you're thinking, "What does all of this have to do with my job? I go to my job and I'm stuck with the rest of the day based on how much time is left when I get home."

Yes, that is the traditional way of looking at your work. For those over forty, I'm proposing a radical new way of looking at your work. You get to design your *entire* day around the work *you* want to do, rather than just the limited time left over after an empty and meaningless day at the office.

Where would you go?

Where would you go for your work? What would be perfect for you?

Would you like to work from home, or would you prefer to work outdoors? Would you prefer to work alone or with others? Maybe you would rather drive a short distance to a small office and work with a small group of other people. Or perhaps you would enjoy working with hundreds of others around you in a large organization.

How about lunch?

When will you eat lunch? Where will you eat lunch? Who will you eat lunch with on a typical day?

Back in my corporate days, I remember sneaking out at lunch to go for a run. I also remember too many lunch hours spent in drab conference rooms, working with others while eating unhealthy food. I can remember thinking how terrible this was for my system.

How long will your work day be?

How long will you work each day? What will you do after work? Who will you spend your time with after work?

This is all part of the design of your perfect vocational day.

How will your evenings go?

When will you eat dinner? Who will you be with at dinner on a typical day? What will you do after dinner? What does your evening look like?

Will you spend the evening alone, with others, or a combination of the two? Your evenings are an important part of your perfect vocational day. This, again, is something most employers don't care at all about, unless you are spending your evenings at the office, of course.

This is the difference between creating the perfect work for you, and just dragging yourself home after a long day at the office and collapsing on the couch.

When you do just a job, the quality of your downtime suffers as you worry about the next day of work.

It's so important to come home to support and love and downtime after your work ends each day. Coming home to someone who does not support the work you love will drain you, and you'll have less energy for your quest for vocational happiness and for the experience of life itself.

What about sleep?

At the end of your perfect vocational day, when will you go to sleep? How will you go to sleep? What nightly ritual will you follow before bed? A little yoga, a warm bath, light reading, television, or intimacy with someone you love?

What's perfect for me?

You must keep asking yourself this question, because no one else will do it for you. Be careful as you design your perfect vocational day, because you will indeed start to move towards it. Make sure you really know just what you want.

Typical job searching is backwards

Most people look for jobs that are available with little thought to all the other hours of their days. The typical job description only covers the requirements of the job. I have never seen one that covers whether you should exercise or eat a big breakfast.

The point is: It's critical to design what you want *before* you go looking for it.

Now you get to play by new rules

After many years of playing the work game the traditional way, now you get to change the rules. When you design the work day you want, you automatically start to alter your thinking, and you start to focus on what you want and what you do not want.

Place your focus on what you want. Don't focus too much on what you don't want in your work life, or this is exactly what you'll end up with.

Now at work

Once at work, what exactly will you do? What activities will align your abilities and your interests and bring you the most joy?

Joy?

Yes, joy! Now that's a question no one in the Human Resources department will ever ask you about. This is where you must be specific.

Your mind can't tell the difference between what is real and what is imagined when envisioning a work day that will bring you joy. You must create the reality you seek.

What are you working on?

Are you developing software, making sandwiches, teaching math, painting, speaking, doing financial analysis, taking pictures, or promoting a new cosmetic product?

What would give you the most joy in your work? What would leave you breathless? What would make Monday your best day of the week and Friday the worst because you have to wait until Monday to resume your beloved work?

What work could you do now and continue to do until you stop breathing?

Why retiring will lead you to a quick death

The other day I received the enrollment package for AARP (American Association for Retired People) in the mail. This really scared me. I thought perhaps I was now in the group of those getting ready to retire and die. Soon I would be bombarded with sales calls about anti-aging creams, Hawaii vacations, and term-life plans.

This only increased the sense of urgency I felt about my life's work and my calling. I decided I needed this work to emerge through me now — before the retirement product sales calls started coming!

Most Americans after forty do not like their work, let alone love it. They dream, instead, of one day retiring, and then finally doing what they enjoy. The problem with this strategy is that life tends to get in the way while you make long range plans.

After forty, crises will hit — it's only a matter of when. If you are doing what you love, you have the best kind of health insurance. When your crisis hits, your work will give you the strength to ride out the storm, and then recover quickly.

You need to be specific

What are you working on that will last a lifetime? Whether you are working for yourself or someone else, the questions are the same.

What specific products or services are you offering in your perfect day of work? What are the features of each of these services? What are the benefits to others of what you are offering? Who are the ideal customers for your services? Day in and day out for the rest of your life, what type of people do you want to work with? Are they engineers, students, disabled children, artists, or advertising representtatives?

Until you are clear about what you want, you and your work will continue to be mismatched.

Now what?

Now you have the vision of your perfect vocational day. Is this a daily pattern you could follow for the rest of your life? Good!

Now you can start to examine how to close the gap between your new vision and today.

For some of you, this will come easy. For others, years of external negative influences, and perhaps a little fear, might prevent quick action, and your next steps might have to be small.

The important part is that you start

Little steps turn into bigger steps. New possibilities turn into bigger possibilities. You are unique and special, and you have many gifts to offer the world.

With a new vision of what would be just perfect for you, you can begin to create the second half of your life and work in a way that includes what is most important to you. As you plan your perfect vocational day, you will have begun moving down the path to an authentic life.

Can't I just separate my life from my work?

This is just an excuse for not moving forward, and deep down, you know this is not possible. I wish it were, but it's not. Your work and what you do impacts your health, your sense of self, your relationships with others, and your overall happiness.

Isn't it worth taking just a little extra time to think about your perfect work life?

Before turning forty, we needed jobs and careers to build both our ego and our sense of self. After forty, jobs and careers are both limiting and outdated.

A new sense of urgency

After forty when your crisis hits — and it will — you will have a new sense of urgency about your life and what to do with it. Your work, and what you do each and every day, is a great place to start.

Turning work into vocation

Evaluate where you have been in your life and ask yourself, "Is this enough?"

Any day is a great time to reevaluate your life and plans.

What would you do with free time?

If you had a day to yourself, what would you do and why?

The answer to this question may provide the answers you are seeking for vocational happiness.

What inspires you and why?

Who inspires you? What stories, books, and movies inspire you?

Other people and their work can encourage you to seek your own true vocational path.

How long could you take to make your change?

If you quit your unfulfilling job today, how long could you go without making an income? Would it be one month, six months, one year? How could you lengthen your time? The more time you can allow yourself, the better.

Ask the right question

Your authentic life starts with finally asking the question, "What would my perfect work be?"

Grade yourself

Is your work life significant?

Does your work provide meaning?

Is your work fulfilling?

Does your work make sense to you?

Do you find joy in your work?

Only you can grade your work life.

Don't wait

Don't wait for your spouse or your boss or your kids or society to give you approval. The permission to start to create and live your perfect vocational day must come from within yourself.

Your approval muscle just takes use and practice.

Envision a better future

Many times, your mind can't tell the difference between what you imagine and what is real, when thinking about the future. This is good news when you start to envision your perfect vocational day.

Feed your mind with new — and more fulfilling — ideas.

Do you feel alive each day, or are you just surviving?

How is your energy each day? Do you wake up fully alert and ready to work?

Do you jump out of bed each morning at the thought of starting work?

Does your mind race during the night because you can't wait to get up in the morning?

Before going to bed, do you get excited just thinking of the work that you get to do the next day?

Much better to jump out of bed than to need a push to get out.

Listen to your loved ones

How are you feeling about your loved ones? Are you supportive and always ready to listen to them in a calm and supportive way?

When you are doing what you love, you will have more patience for the people you love.

Do you have JUST a job?

Is yours "just a job," with empty days and wasted staff meetings? Does it seem like it's always all about the money? Does your employer have a "what have you done for me lately?" attitude toward you and your work? Does it seem like you don't have control of your work, and what you do? Do you feel trapped?

The only way out of job prison is to find the key yourself.

Purpose

Find a purpose for your life.

If you don't, you will end up with someone else's dream life.

New beliefs

Replace old beliefs that are no longer useful to you.

If you believe you are not smart enough, for example, start believing you are just as smart as anybody else.

Now, that was easy, wasn't it?

Passion

What activities get you most excited about life?

This is a great time to re-create your life for more fulfillment, more joy, and more happiness in your work and life. What can you do today to get started?

Twenty secrets for finding your perfect work

OK, these may not be secrets anymore, and they will be hard work — and they will be worth the trouble.

Follow the steps in order and spend quality, quiet thinking time with each one. Take as much time as you need with each step.

Take a deep breath and get started. I'll be cheering you on each step of the way.

Step 1: Find a purpose for your life. (Otherwise you will end up living someone else's dream.)

Step 2: Figure out what bothers you most about the world and do something about it. This is the best path towards authentic work, and it can start in your own neighborhood.

Step 3: Determine what is most important to you. Most of us live our lives around what others tell us is most important.

Step 4: Align your new goals around what is most important. These will become the roadmap for your life's direction.

Step 5: Have a healthy perspective of yourself. When you feel good about yourself, everything else just seems to fall into place.

Step 6: Replace old beliefs that are no longer useful to you. If you believe that everything you touch fails, for example, start believing you are a success, and think of examples that prove it.

Step 7: Create new possibilities for your life. Others will help you create new *impossibilities*; there is a big difference.

Step 8: Figure out who you want to be when you grow up. It's never too late to start redefining your life and your sense of self.

Step 9: Practice living the life you want now. You won't believe it's possible until you actually do something.

Step 10: Figure out what you are passionate about. Start by thinking about the activities that make you most excited about life.

Step 11: Align your abilities and your interests. This is the quickest path to vocational passion.

Step 12: What would a perfect vocational day be for you? My perfect vocational day, for example, includes writing this book for you.

Step 13: Write your autobiography five years from today. When you write down the life you want to live and read it, magical things happen to close the gap.

Step 14: Downscale your lifestyle now to create the opportunities that you seek. Sorry, this is a mandatory step — you need to have a lighter backpack for the next part of your life.

Step 15: Strengthen your relationships and support systems. Again, this is a brave but necessary step: you must shed the people in your life who do not share your dreams, and nurture relationships with new people who are excited about your journey.

Step 16: Grow strong emotionally. You must learn to ignore the opinions of others — even those who love you — if they don't mesh with your dream.

Step 17: Give yourself permission to follow your heart. Tell yourself it's OK to be selfish. It's your life.

Step 18: Laugh a lot and enjoy the ride. The process of discovery and trial and error are part of the path.

Step 19: Live with integrity as a path towards an authentic life. Define what integrity means to you and then follow your own rules.

Step 20: Eat well, exercise, and get plenty of sleep. This will give you that extra bounce in your step.

Finding your life's work — the work that's just perfect for you — must start and finish with you. Use these twenty secrets; they will get you there.

Rosemary bounces back

Rosemary was so unhappy with her work that she simply couldn't take it anymore. That's when she started to pursue her perfect vocational day.

She had been out of work during the height of the worst California unemployment in years. She had been laid off the day she returned from maternity leave after having her third child. Rosemary felt hurt that no one wanted an IT systems administrator. It did not seem to matter that she had the education, expertise, and people skills. She was close to the point of despair.

Rosemary needed a plan. She was not going to find my destination if she did not know where she was going. During her vocational journey, Rosemary explored what her goals were, what she wanted to do, and more importantly, what she needed to do to get to her goals.

Rosemary figured out that she wanted to work; at this point she did not care what she would be doing as long as she was not at home with her three kids.

Rosemary loves her children dearly, but she learned during her time at home that she was not meant to stay at home. Rosemary found a job as a contractor working for a large computer company, five minutes from her house. She was very pleased, but she knew this contract job was only a pit-stop in her vocational journey — not her destination.

Through her discovery and reflection and a little coaching, Rosemary mustered the courage to subject herself to yet another interview.

Since Rosemary was putting together a roadmap, she kept applying for jobs knowing that she wanted to continue working with computers, but she did not want the stress that goes along with the role in most companies.

Her passion was to one day work near the ocean. To her surprise, she was contacted by a company that does Marine Research. She had submitted her resume five months earlier, so she was no longer expecting to hear from them.

This job was her destination, at least for this part of her journey. She was positive, but also fearful. Would they like her? Would she make her usual mistakes in the interview? Would she say the wrong things?

With coaching, Rosemary was able to envision herself in the position, facing her fear of failure, and refocusing on what she should concentrate on — the job requirements.

Rosemary got the job, and she knew in her heart that encouragement and support were key components in her success in obtaining this position.

These days Rosemary is grateful every day, as she walks to her office. She works right next to the ocean — a dream come true. She gets to do the work she loves (work with computers, research, and design) in a low-stress environment that helps keep her sanity.

Rosemary believes she is very close to her *perfect vocational day*. And now she is a great believer in seeking her vocational *passion*.

Lessons to learn

Achieving your perfect vocational day is possible if you keep the dream — the vision — of exactly what you want to be doing alive. The more specific the vision, the better.

Rosemary knew inside why her job criteria were important to her, and that helped drive her momentum. Rosemary discovered that once she was true to herself, everything else seemed to fall into place. This takes courage and risk-taking and internal motivation. You will almost never get approval from someone else; you must give this gift to yourself.

Having the initial vision is key. Having a clear picture of exactly what your perfect vocational day will be is the first step. It is important to be specific and honest with yourself. Design a life that works for you. You get to call the shots and create an inspiring vision that drives you forward.

With a clear vision of what would be just perfect for you, you are ready for true joy and happiness in your work. You will benefit, and so will everyone around you.

Present

Closing the gap between where you are and what you want

What are you doing in the present to move towards your perfect vocational day? Do you know what the gap is between your dreams and where you are now? Do you know the real reason why reaching your perfect vocational day is so important to you?

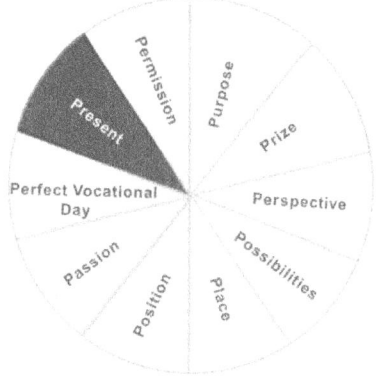

It is difficult to close the gap without a clear vision of where you are going.

When you clearly define your desired state and compare it with your present state, it becomes clear what gaps need to be closed to make progress towards discovering and doing more of what you want to do when it comes to your life's work.

There will be major challenges that will come up at this phase. Your relationships might come under stress. Your emotional strength might be tested.

Your feeling of financial stability might feel jeopardized. With a strong desired state — what you want and why — you will be ready for this journey toward your authentic life.

What to do right now

Look at the big picture of your life. This can be hard to do. The daily pressures of a thankless job, a demanding commute, and mounting bills all lead to stress. Worst of all is the nagging feeling that your life is out of your control, and slowly slipping away.

"I don't have time to change"

I hear this a lot. While it's normal, this is just an excuse, and you know it. Most people don't fear change, but how the change might upset their dull and comfortable lives.

Are you feeling alive about your work?

Do you pinch yourself because you can't believe you've figured out a way to actually do what you love *and* make the income you need?

If not, you still have work to do!

This is possible for you

You need a plan. It starts with what you want. Most of us start with what we don't want, and that is exactly what we end up with.

Let's say you have one of those corporate jobs. You're making good money, and your in-laws are proud of you.

But each day, it's getting harder and harder to go to work. Work pressures are rising; you constantly work under the fear that you are not living up to their expectations.

It's time to become a free agent

Whether you intend to work for yourself or someone else, the steps are the same. What are the services and products you could sell to someone else, and that you most want to deliver or create?

This is a helpful exercise even if you plan to work for someone else.

For each service or product, write down the features.

For example, if you want to deliver customer service training, one feature might be interactive or customer-driven education.

What are the benefits?

The next step is to identify — next to each feature — how someone would benefit from your product or service. For example, the benefit of customer-driven classroom education might be that it is real-time and instructor-lead, resulting in fast-paced, hands-on learning.

Who would be your ideal niche audience?

Who, specifically, do you want to serve as your customers? Are they middle-aged men, college students, executives, pet owners?

Normally we take jobs, and then we have to live with the culture we walk into. There is a better model. You start by deciding what type of customer you most want to serve.

For example, if you really want to serve college students, going to work for the Social Security Administration might not be the best choice.

You create your work

This is the mental shift you must make. You design exactly what would be just perfect for you.

Consider all the services or products you could offer to others.

You deserve it

Now, over forty and having worked fifteen to twenty years, this is your time to finally design your life the way you want it.

What about the money?

A complicated subject, and unique to each person.

Think about how much you need, not how much you want. There is a difference. How can you lighten your backpack now?

Can your spouse work? Can you find a spouse who would work? Can your family help you plan some cutbacks in the short term? Can you cash in your retirement fund — you won't need it. After all, the only people who retire are those who don't love what they do.

Can you live on less material happiness, and more internal bliss?

What about my responsibilities?

We all have responsibilities. Whether you are single and live alone, or married with three kids, you have responsibilities.

But if you are over forty, this is the time to be selfish. Gather the team together, and ask for their support.

You don't intend to stop being responsible; you just need, at this time of your life, to be more creative in how you earn the money so you can be happier and more fulfilled in your life. You just need a better way to make your life work for you.

The choice is always up to you

You can ignore this advice, and continue to waste your time and energy on useless work while your life moves on.

Or instead, you can decide right now: enough is enough. You can realize that the only thing holding you back is *you*. You can decide and take action to change to work you are passionate about, and that better aligns your natural abilities and interests.

Be a role model

The best role model you can provide for your kids, or those you love, is to do the work you are passionate about.

This is the authentic life. It will be a lonely pursuit at first (well, I'll be cheering for you), but soon you will wonder why you waited so long to change in the first place.

Stressed about your job?

No need — you have bigger plans now to work on.

The difference between "need" and "want"

Let's face it: Most people spend too much money on things they don't really need. The more money we make, the more we tend to spend. This endless cycle of materialism has led many people to confuse the word "need" with the word "want." As in, "we need a big-screen TV for our new home theater." Or, "I need a new pair of shoes to go with my new outfit."

If you want to achieve your vocational passion, and you get to do the work that makes you want to jump out of bed every day because you can't wait to go to work, then you need to reorder your priorities. Stay away from the purely material.

The pursuit of material success is often the root cause of burnout at mid-life. In fact, a recent study at the University of California at Berkeley found that people primarily motivated by the love of their work grow dissatisfied as they begin to make more money.

The first step to breaking free from the materialism trap is to understand the difference between "need" and "want."

We need food, clothing, shelter, reliable transportation, education, enrichment, and the technology necessary to do our work. Also, we need the occasional small indulgence to treat our children and ourselves.

We do not need 500 cable TV channels, brand new luxury cars, 5,000-square-foot homes in exclusive neighborhoods, lavish ski vacations, and smart phones that do everything but think for us.

There is nothing wrong with wanting these things. But understand that these things do not make us happy, in and of themselves. And, they are often links in the chains that bind us to jobs we despise.

Often, those who make a leap to vocational passion end up making more money over the long term. But in the short term, income usually declines. It may even go away for a period of time. Typically, the first two years of a career change — in particular, one motivated purely by vocational passion — are financially difficult. Major lifestyle and attitude adjustments are critical to making the money last while you pursue your dream.

The amazing thing is that once you learn to live on less, it becomes a habit. The peace of mind that comes from relying less on materialism to define success usually leads to a greater and deeper happiness.

Getting real about money

Now that we understand that pursuing vocational passion requires a major adjustment in our attitude toward money and material comfort, the next step is getting down to the details.

What does it take to transform yourself and your family from a unit that consumes as much as it earns to one that respects money and makes it last?

The trick is to look at all expenses, both big and small. Leave no stone unturned. No saving is too small, and no category of spending should escape scrutiny.

Those looking to leave a job to pursue their vocational passion face two core issues: raising enough money to fund a career change, and changing spending patterns to make the money last.

Raising the money can be a tremendous challenge, depending on your financial resources. Savings, bonds, securities, IRAs, home equity, jewelry, valuables, and family resources are all avenues for raising capital to sustain your family during this transition.

Consider the following options to cut down your burn rate. Some will seem dramatic. But if you have decided that your only chance at happiness is to pursue a vocational dream, small measures won't cut it.

- If you live in a mansion, consider selling it. You could use the proceeds to buy a smaller house in a less expensive neighborhood. That could leave you with no mortgage or at least a much smaller payment each month. Whatever the size of your home, you can go a step further and use 100% of the proceeds of a home sale as working cash for the transition, and then rent a house instead. Seeking the advice of a tax attorney or a financial planner may be wise, particularly when you are selling your home or using it as security on a loan. But, do not let these advisers sway you from your core decisions. They are there only to give you advice on the smartest way to pursue the path you have chosen.

- Consider part-time or project-based work in the field you are moving out of to supplement your income during the transition. Also, look to part-time work as a way to slow your burn rate. Ask each eligible member of your family to contribute toward supporting the household.

- Evaluate your home, car, and health insurance costs. Are you over-insured? Can you raise your deductibles? This can often reduce premiums significantly. Also, health insurance rates for small businesses, even those with one or two employees, are often more favorable than individual policies.
- Take a look at what you drive. Is it a "badge" brand imported car? Is it a "suburban assault vehicle"? There are many presentable, economical cars with good long-term reliability that can be purchased used. Sell your status symbol and buy one of these other cars instead. You will save on car payments, gas, and insurance. You will be better off the minute you stop trying to impress people with what you drive.
- Let your children fund a little more of their own college education. Student loans are not a lifelong burden. Many successful people have paid for their education this way, and so can your children. They will still love you.
- Sweat the small stuff. Look at every element of your daily spending and ask whether it is necessary. Do you have features on your phone service that you never use? How many videos do you rent every week? (They are free at the local library, by the way.) How important are those premium cable channels?
- How much do you spend on eating out and junk food? How many pizzas did you order last month? How much do you spend every day on designer coffee, soft drinks, and fast

food? How much do you spend on dinners at nice restaurants? Take a look at what's in your grocery cart. How much of it is snack food or impulse buys that are both bad for you and a waste of money?

- If you still need a reason to quit smoking, the five dollar-plus per pack you are spending ought to finally get you to give up that habit.
- Look at how your home runs: Is your home well-insulated, or does money in the form of energy fly out the windows? Do you turn out the lights when you leave a room? How much do you waste each year on late fees for credit cards or overdue videos? How necessary is each short trip you take in the car? Can you combine trips, or make small, local errands on foot or on your bike (which saves money and burns calories)?

Make the effort to evaluate everything you do. You'll be amazed by the amount of money you can save.

Where do you want to contribute?

What issues concern you the most? Where do you feel your natural gifts and talents can make the most difference in the world? Do you want to help children learn, feed the elderly, or help others with their financial problems?

The choice is yours. There are countless opportunities and choices to make in how we'll spend our time during the second half of our lives.

Each choice we make will bring change and energy into our lives, while attracting what we are seeking.

This is your time to shine, and share your natural gifts with the world. Contributing in the areas of your life that interest you most is the best way to live an authentic second half. Where exactly do you want to contribute now?

What is most important to you?

What does your list of "most important" look like? Family, health, developing products, painting, helping families in need, traveling?

You need to make an honest assessment of what is most important in your life now. If you are like most people, before forty this list was driven largely by external expectations.

This new assessment needs to be an internal list driven by what you are most passionate about. What does your list look like? Can you think of how you might align your life's work around what is most important to you right now?

Notice that I said your "life's work." This is the difference between *just* a job and a vocation.

When your work reflects what is most important to you, you never need to retire (get ready to be tired) — your life's work stays with you until you stop breathing.

What could you do for as long as you are breathing?

Answering this question will change the way you think about your life and your work.

How do you feel about you?

Notice your feelings about you. Take a step back, and in your mind's eye, examine yourself from a distance. What do you notice? What do you love most about you? What areas would you like to change, and why? If you know the why, you can always figure out the "how" part later.

The way you feel about yourself will have an impact on your emotions, which will impact on your thoughts, and on your body, right down to your individual cells. Those around you will feel the impact as well.

Continue to focus on the areas you are most proud of, and make a commitment to change the areas that cause you concern.

The better you feel about yourself, the better everyone around you will look as well, and you will attract more of what you seek in your life.

Corral your brain synapses

Have you noticed that when you think a thought, you immediately start to think other, similar thoughts? Most of the time, we think a negative thought and then, before we know it, we start thinking more, similar negative thoughts. This is - how the brain works.

Remember: you are the person running your wonderful brain. Start now to think of new possibilities for your work and your life. Do you want now, after forty, to become a brain surgeon, build boats, open a deli, or teach fourth grade?

Why not? It only takes new possibilities, and new possibilities can happen with new thinking.

What work best fits you now?

In your second half of life, this is a much better question to ask.

Those silly job descriptions you used to try to fit yourself into don't work after forty. Now, it is much better to ask yourself what work best fits you. What work feels just right to you? Can you think of work that will be challenging to accomplish, and for which you also have the abilities and interests?

What work makes you feel alive and joyful?

Sometimes, just like trying on new clothes, you have to try on new kinds of work. Just as your body has changed, after forty your skills and priorities are a little different than they were when you were twenty-five.

What are you most passionate about now?

What are you most passionate about? What things or activities give you the most energy and excitement, and leave you breathless for more?

This is a great place to start. For example, does yoga make you feel so great, you just wish it would never end? Well, write down all the ideas you can come up with around yoga as your work.

Here's a question I get all the time (many people seem to think this will stump me): "What if I am passionate about sex?"

Well, great. Think of all the people in the world who have similar passions and interests around sex.

You could be an educator, a healer, a facilitator, and there are countless products to sell in this area.

The point is that no subject you are passionate about should be off-limits, as long as it is legal, and doesn't harm others or the environment.

Start with a short list of your passions. Walk around all day with this list, and just reflect and look around you — you will get many ideas.

What would your perfect day be like?

This is a great exercise to try. Make a list, and imagine you could create a new typical day for yourself — one that you would be excited to repeat over and over again for the rest of your life. Start with when you wake, and plan it right through to when you go to sleep. How will your day go, and what will you do? Who will you be with?

Be careful, as the mind doesn't know the difference between what is real and imagined when you think about your future. Whatever perfect day you write down, you will start to move towards it.

What can I do today?

Take small steps. Ensure that you are emotionally strong for this journey. You will need to stop caring what others think. Make sure those people close to you are supportive. If they are not, you will have to build up a better support team around you.

Think about money. How much money do you actually need as compared to how much you want? There is a difference. Do you have a big retirement fund? I have great news! Now that you have decided to find your life's work, you will never need to retire. Cash in that retirement fund now and use it. You will disappoint your financial advisors, but you will enhance your sense of control by deciding how you will use your money now.

Give yourself permission

Sometimes this is all it takes. Have you ever made a personal decision and immediately felt better? Well, this is exactly what you can do now with your work.

Give yourself permission now to not settle for anything less than a joyful, passionate, authentic second half of life.

You will never look back.

Economic crisis: what to do about it

Not since the Great Depression of 1929 have we seen such a financial crisis, and frankly, the lack of national leadership that we are experiencing now.

Banks are failing, and Wall Street greed and the chase after quick money have finally caused this country to grind to a financial halt. All Americans are worried now — from those with money, wondering how much their nest eggs will shrink, to those who need the money in their bank account just to live each month.

My guess is that a majority of Americans, especially those of us over forty, are worried about simply making ends meet month to month. The challenge of whether to pay the car insurance, make the car payment, or simply buy food for the family, becomes a trade-off every month.

Sleepless nights over credit

Many people in this country didn't sleep well last night, lying awake worrying about whether it was more important to avoid being late on their payments (letting their credit slip), or to buy food and pay the electric bill to keep the house warm. I would guess that the last thing on anyone's mind right now is how to do the work they love for the rest of their lives.

Of the seventy million plus Americans between forty and sixty-five, my guess is that more than half don't love their work, let alone like it. In fact, many dislike their work, and even just *having* to go to work each day, while worrying about keeping their family fed, is causing stress and illness.

The problem is overspending

Many of us have overspent, and the regular biweekly paycheck for the job we dislike barely covers our obligations — and leaves most of us drained at the end of the day. Just this week, in the small city where I live, the local planning department announced plans to lay off half the department. I made a call to offer outplacement services for their employees who would be out of work, but the city representative sadly told me they couldn't afford this service.

The head of this planning department committed suicide just a few days later. He was fifty-five years old, and distraught over the possibility of losing his job, and perhaps his home — it was just too much.

This new crisis must be faced with a sense of urgency

At one level, I wish our leadership was having around-the-clock meetings over the lack of health care for millions of Americans, the out-of-control cost of education, and the homeowner crisis. On the other hand, we have a history of acting quickly without a long range plan.

You need a long range plan when you're over 40

Given the climate of uncertainly, this is the best time of all to make a plan for your life that centers around your work. Over forty, you have probably, on average, another forty years to live — that's half your life. You can, like so many people do, just wait for what life has to offer, but soon, you will wake up and find yourself at fifty, sixty, seventy years old ... and wonder how time moved so fast.

The better alternative

The better alternative is to make a plan for your life around doing the work you love. This is the path to an authentic life full of integrity.

Take, for example, the job you don't like — the one you are doing today — the one that barely pays the bills. Well, one way to start is to move immediately to another, similar low paying job doing what you love!

This doesn't solve your financial problems, but it does start to improve your sense of confidence, self-esteem, and emotional strength.

One of my clients — we'll call him Bill — works as a sales director for a company in the food industry. He has had his current job for ten years, and he just hates it. He travels most of the week, and he doesn't care about the product he sells anymore. To make things even worse, he has a demanding boss.

What should Bill do?

Bill saw the doctor the other day because he is having trouble sleeping. The doctor said not to worry; Bill was just having anxiety attacks. Thanks, Doc!

Bill had very little saved and very little in retirement funds, and is living month to month, so I told him he needed to take action.

After much work getting him thinking about it, Bill told me his greatest passion was reading. He just loved to read, especially history books. Bill never thought he could make this passion his vocation, but it turns out Bill is also quite a good speaker, given his long years as a salesman.

A new beginning for Bill

After much trial and error, today Bill is working on a transition plan. He has decided to go to school at night to get the necessary credentials to become a high school history teacher. This will only pay half of what he requires to maintain his household, so in addition, he has been interviewing with an educational firm that sells textbooks to schools — history textbooks! He can spend two afternoons a week on this role working within his schedule as a teacher, and make up some of the extra income he needs. Bill also found that he loved history so much, he wanted to start a nonprofit firm, and he was even able to get some funding for it. His new firm will provide programs to schools to help children connect with American history.

Bill was very fortunate in having a supportive partner. His wife went back to work part-time in local retail. Her small wage helps to pay the mortgage. Overall, Bill has a new sense of freedom and control over his life. While his economic situation in the short term has not changed, he now has a plan that, with discipline and daily actions, will move him towards an authentic life that will make him happier — and make those around him happier as well.

What can you do?

Negative thinking brings more negativity. Looking at new possibilities will bring new creativity and possibilities into your life. It all starts with a vision. Envision what you want now with regards to your work, and write it down — this is where the magic happens.

Start talking to others about your plan — this commits you to moving forward.

Take small daily steps; measure your progress; learn to celebrate.

Like Bill, you can define a new plan for yourself based on your own situation. Build a sense of urgency now about your life and your work. This will force new decisions, new plans, and new movement toward a better life.

You have many gifts, and the world is waiting for you to offer them.

What are you waiting for? This is the best time ever to stop worrying about the economy and start living a more joyful and fulfilling life centered around your work.

Happiness doesn't have to start or end based on the balance in your checking account. It can start and grow based on the love and joy in your heart. This can occur when you do the work you love — and after forty this is absolutely necessary.

Your life depends on it

Early one morning, Robert awoke, made his wife of forty-one years some banana bread, took out the garbage, and called to cancel a doctor's appointment scheduled for the next day. He wrote a note to remind his wife to pick up the dry cleaning. All things considered, it seemed like a normal day.

Robert had retired four years earlier after nearly forty years doing what he loved in the banking industry, but after retirement, his life took a challenging turn.

While he remained friendly and encouraging to others on the outside, on the inside he was suffering a deepening depression. After retirement, Robert couldn't find anything to replace the meaning and fulfillment that his work had provided him. And this void was slowly killing him.

So on that "normal" morning, Robert cleaned up the kitchen after finishing baking the banana bread. Then he drove himself to the parking lot of the bank where he had worked all those years. After carefully parking and locking his car, he walked into a local store and handed a note to the clerk behind the counter. Then he walked outside and shot himself in the head. He ended his life with one bullet at one p.m. on a blazing sunny day.

Robert was my dad.

Your happiness is your responsibility

A few years ago, when I decided to leave corporate America after twenty-five years, I thought I had learned enough about mid-life and work.

After all, I was in the middle of my PhD research on what happens to mid-life adults when they leave the security of the nest to follow their hearts and their life's calling. I had coined a new term, Vocational Passion, to describe this alignment of passions, abilities, and interests. I had started a new online community at TheVocationalCoach.com, and written a book, *P Is for Perfect: Your Perfect Vocational Day,* in an attempt to boil down this research into a practical ten step model.

Yes, I thought, with my corporate background, various degrees, new clients, new office, workshops, public speaking gigs, and a burning desire to make a difference in the world, I had learned enough.

I was wrong. I soon found that the biggest challenges were still ahead — including the suicide of my father.

I'm still struggling to make sense of my father's death, but I also am finding new strength in my own work, helping others to find meaning and fulfillment in their vocational lives. When my dad lost his purpose for living, he also lost the will to live.

Fortunately, most people don't end their own lives, but many people shoot themselves in the head emotionally, continuing to work at jobs that no longer provide meaning or passion or fulfillment.

It doesn't have to be this way. By telling you this story, I hope lives can be saved. We need to acknowledge that depression may be a symptom of not living a life filled with purpose, meaning, and fulfillment. A call to action is a must.

As the psychologist Carl Jung said, mid-life is a time to listen deeply to your heart. Whether we plan for this or not, mid-life can be a period of transition and reappraisal. More inner questioning can occur.

Career plateaus can be reached during this period, driving a need for internal insight and reflection.

Those who don't invest in time for self-reflection in mid-life may experience increased stress and other distress signals. The sense of crisis may vary from one person to the next. For those who do experience stress, making changes in mid-life is never easy or without challenges.

Can you make the difficult choices?

Making work-related change in mid-life to pursue a dream or passion generates a lot of issues. I have observed in working with my own clients that these issues generally fall into three categories: emotional, relationship, and financial, as illustrated in the three groups of questions that follow:

- **Emotional:** Am I good enough? Can I give myself permission to follow my heart?
- **Relationship:** What will my loved ones say? If they don't agree, do I dare test the relationships or rock the boat at this point in my life? Are my loved ones willing to make this sacrifice with me? What if they are not?
- **Financial:** Despite all the "sound" financial advice to save for retirement, do I instead invest in myself now, perhaps turning my financial world upside down?

These questions will all come up. You will feel selfish, and you may be accused of being self-indulgent or self-absorbed.

Mid-life is a time to be selfish. This isn't about change for its own sake, but change to position yourself for the second half of your life, to be authentic, and to shred external views and norms.

During this time, it doesn't help that society's view is that work is something not necessarily to be enjoyed. Most career theory and research have supported this notion by largely ignoring the enjoyment factor. Even counseling psychology has largely followed the same path. The focus has been on matching skills and available types of work. While this can be helpful for younger adults, in mid-life internal needs, desires, and passions beg for attention.

While society expects those in mid-life to simply roll over and prepare to die or retire (I am not sure which is worse), many in mid-life actually begin to wonder how they can start living. For many, it is a rebirth, with new wisdom and with permission from yourself to follow your heart.

Economic conditions can force people to ignore their inner needs and take jobs they don't like to pay the bills. This only helps you further ignore your inner needs.

Achieving vocational passion requires looking inward to understand what brings you the most enjoyment in your work. As a result, you can begin to understand the relationship between achieving greater meaning, and the integrity with which you choose to conduct your life.

It takes action to follow your vocational passion. I am not convinced that money can buy happiness at mid-life, but I am convinced that happiness can increase the richness in your life. We each get to define what that means.

It starts with a simple re-examination of what you have done, are doing, and might do vocationally in the second half of your life. In mid-life and later, it's critical not to ignore your heart. In mid-life, this may turn out to be the most consistent thing in your life when everything else seems in flux.

Sadly, Robert — my dad — wasn't able to do this.

My wonderful grandmother who lived into her mid-nineties used to always say to me, "Bagel, (that's what she called me) just do what makes you happy."

I think I finally understand what she meant.

Five steps to move to what you want most

There's a famous song lyric that asks: "Is that all there is?"

("Is That All There Is?" was written by Jerry Leiber and Mike Stoller and recorded by Leslie Uggams in 1968 and by Peggy Lee in 1969.)

Every seven seconds, an American turns fifty years old. So there's a good chance this song is running through some of their heads.

The question captures the ennui that many people feel in mid-life. They look up at the clock, see it ticking, and begin counting in their heads all the mountains not climbed, the poems not written, and the songs not sung.

It's time to stop asking this question idly. It's time to apply some analytical thinking to your life and plan how to move from the vocational death grip to vocational passion.

Can you throw off the trappings of success and pursue a lifelong dream of opening a bookstore, or becoming a teacher, an organic farmer, a fishing guide, a cabaret singer, or a freelance writer?

Consider these five initial steps you can take to evaluate your situation. Begin the transition away from the meaningless grind and toward a new life that provides you with energy and fulfillment. This is not an overnight process. But it's a process you can begin today.

Step One: Evaluate your life

Lots of people settle for jobs that pay their bills, but leave them feeling empty. If you want to break out of this trap and find another kind of life, you need to evaluate where you'd like to go. Examine where your passions lie. What are your dreams? When you were young, what did you want to be when you grew up? What would you love to do in your spare time if you had some?

Vocational passion is an alignment of your abilities and interests in a role that gives you unlimited energy and happiness.

On a scale of 1-10, where are you when it comes to vocational passion? A *1* is a living drudgery where you force yourself to your desk every morning and dream about the end of the day. A *10* is a perfect alignment between interests and livelihood.

Too many of us are closer to *1* than *10*. Anything lower than a *5* suggests your working life may be feeding your family, but starving your soul.

Step Two: Envision your future

You may have seen the U.S. Navy ad that asks, "If someone wrote a book about your life, would anyone want to read it?"

Here's your chance to write that book — or at least the outline. Sit down and write a short biography that describes who you are five years from now.

Describe exactly the life you wish to lead, doing work that you love. You will know you're done with the exercise when your heart races with excitement.

Then imagine and write down your vision of a perfect vocational day.

It's difficult to achieve something that you have not clearly envisioned. Make sure your vision has clarity. Then document it and pull it out regularly, to refresh your desire to achieve that vision.

Step Three: Tune out negative feedback

Understand this: The moment you announce plans to make a radical change in your life, many people will feel threatened, and they will not wish you well. They will try to talk you out of it, and tell you what a big mistake you're about to make.

Never let the naysayers dictate your life. People who listen to negative voices end up with the status quo.

Step Four: Shore up your support network

Anyone making a change needs supportive friends, and lots of them. I suggest a three-tier model for analyzing your personal support network. This will help you analyze who will be there for you, emotionally and materially, when you make the leap to pursue your vocational passion.

The bottom tier — tier 3 — is made up of the "interested." This tier includes people who take interest in your work and who tend to encourage and follow up with you. These are supportive, but not always directly helpful friends.

The second tier — the "supporters" — includes those who not only take an interest in your work, but who come up with creative ideas to help you move forward. These are friends who put energy into helping you.

Tier one — the "believers" — includes your most active supporters. These people provide tangible assistance by handing out your materials or by telling others about your work. Tier one people will send you new opportunities.

(More about this later.)

Step Five: Assess your risk

When taking action to follow your passion, decide which of the following four financial categories you fall into. Each category requires a different strategy.

Category One: Plenty of money and plenty of time

People in this category have a high tolerance for risk based on their relatively young age and solid financial means. The best strategy for people in this category is to travel, and meet and talk to new people who do what they aspire to do.

Category one mid-lifers should develop plans, experiment, and take big risks.

Category Two: Plenty of money and little time

Because of failing health or advancing age, those in category two have some risk tolerance, but they probably lack a solid support network. Most of their friends will advise against change because they are "too old" or "too sick." People in this category have no time to delay. They must throw themselves into doing what they love.

If you are in this category, get moving. It can only improve your health and your perception of aging.

Category Three: Little time and little money

I define "little money" as having less than six months cash reserves in the bank. Risk tolerance is low in this category, and supporters are probably hard to come by. Most people are in this category.

The best approach if you are in this category is to develop new plans and back-up plans, and take some calculated risks now. For some of you, downsizing to a smaller house and cashing in the IRA might be a good way to jumpstart the plan.

For others, taking smaller steps works better. Go back to school to learn new skills, or switch to a job where you'll work with people who are more aligned with what you love.

Category Four: No money and no time

I define "no money" as less than three months cash reserves in the bank.

People in this position have a very low risk tolerance. They will find little support to help them move toward doing what they love.

The best course for you if you are in this category is to find something that immediately gets you closer to your passion.

For example: Say you love animals, but you work as a software engineer. You could choose to work in a pet store and take a drastic interim cut to your standard of living. If this doesn't fit for you, you could take a job at a pet-related company or industry.

In the short term, the move allows you to spend time with people who are more likely to share your interests and values.

What's the worst that can happen?

Remember this: *You won't die or become homeless if you pursue what you love.*

You may, however, find that your relationship to your money changes. You will respect money more, and you'll find that you can manage on less of it.

Also understand that pursuing your vocational passion doesn't always mean making less money. But it does mean that money is not the only consideration — or even the most important consideration — in choosing your new vocational path.

Give yourself permission to move toward your passion now. Realize that your current relationships may be tested. Be prepared for obstacles. Don't let your progress stall. Life is too precious.

Even if you don't act to pursue your vocational passion, every seven seconds someone else will come along and ask themselves: "Is that all there is?"

Many of them will answer, "No," and will do something about it. You can be one of the doers.

The top 10 ways to quit your job

1 Figure out why you should quit in the first place

That's right. If you find joy, passion, and meaning in your work, there is no reason to quit.

Sadly, this isn't the case for many of the people I meet.

Look at what is most important to you. Is your work aligned with what you prize most in your life? If not, this is a good reason to change now. Does your job pay the bills, but not feed your soul? This is another good reason to quit.

Do you find it hard to drag yourself out of bed in the morning? Yet another reason to quit.

2 Find new authentic ways to earn what you need

How can you earn income working at activities that seem like a better alignment of your abilities and your interests? What work can you do that will last a lifetime? What kind of work gives you the most passion and joy? What work excites you? What work helps you live with integrity and is the most natural expression of who you are?

3 Stop fooling yourself

I have heard all the excuses: the work is unfulfilling, but I have a family to support; I have bills to pay; doing what I love isn't realistic or practical; I have been doing this job too long to quit now.

The better question to ask is: "How *can* I support my family and pay my bills by doing work that feeds my soul, and that I love to do?"

What a concept!

You'll appreciate your family even more. Even paying your bills won't seem so bad.

4 Uncross your arms

Stop being so negative!

The more reasons you create to explain why you can't make your dreams come true, the more you'll believe what's *not* possible in your life. And then you'll simply drag yourself back to that office for more useless paperwork, meetings, performance reviews, too many emails and worst of all — those office birthday celebrations.

5 Don't give up

Brain synapses work in a powerful way. You think a thought, and you can't help but to think new, similar thoughts. So as you think of a new possibility in your work — doing what you love — you think of a solution you never considered before.

Be careful what you think; don't concentrate on not thinking about it, either — the opposite is also true.

For example, right now, do *not* think of a green door.

You're thinking about a green door, aren't you?

You see; to *not* think of a green door, you first have to think of a green door!

6 Ask better questions

Vocational passion takes new muscles. To help prepare, start to ask better questions. For example, as you think about your life's work, ask yourself:

"Do you realize that…?"

As your mind races for an answer, new ideas emerge. As you think about your life right now, finish these sentences:

"I am grateful for…"

"Isn't it great that…?"

These questions will help to get new positive emotions flowing.

7 Build a better support network

The more time you spend around those who are stagnant in their work lives, the more stuck you will also feel. Start now to spend time with those people who have the same passions as you do, and you'll gain new energy in your life.

8 Rethink your definition of success

The more you measure your work and life success using external factors such as great pay, great performance reviews, a big office, a large staff, a great job title, and proud in-laws (the worst measure of all), the more pressure you'll feel to continually raise the bar to live up to these expectations.

These expectations are totally out of your control.

9 Make a decision and then take action

There were three frogs sitting on three lily pads, and two frogs decided to jump. How many frogs were left on the lily pads?

This will be the most important and most useful math lesson you will ever learn.

(All three frogs were still sitting there because two had only *decided*, and no one had taken action.)

#10 Treat your money with more respect

When you work at *just* a job, you don't really appreciate what you make. You just want more of it, hoping it will somehow make up for your unhappiness at work. You don't even appreciate it when you spend it. Again, you just want to buy more stuff to make up for your unhappiness.

The good news is that when you earn money doing the work you love, every dollar you earn and spend takes on more meaning and satisfaction.

Quit your job: Rejoin your life instead

Jobs lead to careers, which lead to retirement, and then death.

You can work at your *vocation* (the work that calls you) forever — until the day you stop breathing.

When you are doing work that you love, you won't see the difference between work and play. The only people who retire (retreat and get ready to "tire") are those who do not love what they do.

With vocational passion — doing the work you love — the concept of saving and or putting off your work happiness for after retirement won't make sense to you anymore.

So when you get those AARP (retirement fund) notices in the mail, run in the other direction!

You can and should make better use of your life and your work now. You'll be happier, and the people who love you will be happier, too.

Isn't this enough?

Mid-life Monica picked up a paintbrush

Walking out into the garden, Monica Lee gathered some bright yellow daffodils and deep violet irises. She plucked some greens, stuck them in with the blooms, looked up at the blue sky, and gave thanks for another beautiful day. Glancing at her wetsuit stretched out in the sun to dry after an hour of boogie boarding in ocean temperatures of fifty-five degrees, Monica smiled. "This is the best time of my life," she whispered to herself as a soft breeze gently ruffled her long silver blonde hair.

She gazed at her reflection in the window and noticed she was still wearing her leotards after an hour of yoga.

It was nearly nine a.m., time to take Char Lee, her new German Shepherd puppy, for a walk. Upon their return, Monica planned to jump into the shower and sip a tall cool glass of orange juice. After this mentally and physically energizing ritual, she would be prepared to face her easel. Today's challenge would be to give it life by designing her painting, "Scene of a village in the South of France."

Having raised four children, the eldest nearing forty, Monica was now just two years shy of her sixtieth birthday, and a grandmother of ten. Looking back in time to her earlier years, she couldn't help thinking how much she had grown and changed throughout the decades. Never would Monica have imagined the bliss and motivational surge she is experiencing at this time of her life.

At forty, Monica picked up a paintbrush for the first time. Not long after that, she was transferring her thoughts and feelings to canvas and selling her paintings worldwide. With maturity, she realized it was of little importance how others perceived her work. Instead, what really mattered was how much she enjoyed putting color and form on canvas. The fact that others responded to her art in such a delightful and positive manner, Monica believed, was a true blessing.

Today Monica enjoys creating for the many Mo Van collectors worldwide, not because she considers herself a great artist, but because God has given her the ability to create for and resonate with all those art lovers who feel and actually live the joy with which the works were inspired and painted.

Monica opened her own gallery, but the uncertainty of making ends meet each month led her to sleep in the back, in a makeshift bed. She showered under a backyard hose and laundered her clothes by hand while she rented her home for the summer to supplement her income as an artist.

She had been financially comfortable, but Monica traded it all for the insecurity of owning her own gallery. She had to follow her dream — she just had to design and live her own *perfect vocational day*.

She had to paint even if her studio was a small, dark hole in the wall, and she had to sell her works globally.

"Doing" never scared her — but not doing terrified Monica.

After the age of fifty, the ocean enticed Monica to heed its call once again. She spent many summers as a young surfer riding the tumultuous waves, and she was reunited with the foamy surf after years away from it. She acquired a boogie board, braided her hair, slipped into a wetsuit, and at fifty-seven years young became a boogie boarder.

No one asks to experience cancer, or the grueling treatments that are part of the healing process. Cancer is unwanted; something that comes upon you like a flash of lightning. Monica could say it stole a year of her life. Instead, she chooses to believe it added life to her years. She could talk about the aches and pains of growing older, but she enjoys instead telling about the joy of having a new puppy lick her face for the first time in her life. She could tell you getting up at night when he needs to relieve himself isn't fun, yet she would rather convey the joy in watching her little pup run to her, happily wagging his tail when his business is finished; waiting for Monica to pat his silky little head and tell him "you're a good boy."

In Monica's philosophy of growing older, we can choose to experience and share our joys and accomplishments, rather than dwelling on our sorrows and regrets, and allowing them to cloud some of the wonderful moments we could be living.

Monica looks in the mirror and likes what she sees. Why? Because she sees herself as a source of inspiration to all she meets. She wants to encourage and empower. Monica wants to motivate and inspire. Life after fifty can be an enlightening and gratifying experience.

The years have given Monica the wisdom to choose the right path and the courage to continue her still adventure-filled journey.

There isn't anything she will not attempt, and it doesn't matter whether she succeeds or not. What matters is that she gave it her best effort — that she actually did it!

Lessons to learn

It is never too late to follow your heart and do authentic work. In many ways, this search will be the most challenging job you have ever done. It takes discipline, a plan, and daily action; not unlike a typical job search.

The journey towards vocational passion and an authentic life, however, requires creativity, inner confidence, and the determination to never give up.

Monica could have listened to others and simply given up. There were many reasons to choose from: health, age, and lack of opportunities — the list is endless.

What is most important is that she refused to give up or listen to others. As result, Monica is now living a life that is richer than she ever imagined.

Permission

Look for the defining moments in your life

Take the time now to examine the beliefs you hold about yourself. Replace old beliefs that are no longer useful to you with new ones that you will need on your journey.

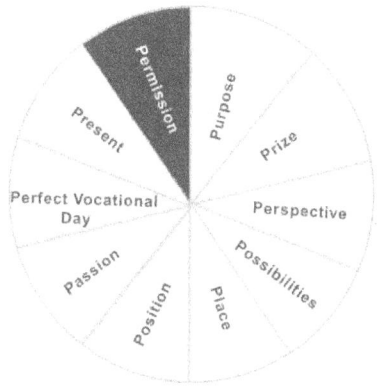

In your forties, there will be a crisis: It might be a major crisis or a small one. Use these trying events as opportunities to create a more fulfilling and authentic life. Build a support network that you can bring along with you on this new journey.

Most important, give yourself permission now to follow your heart. This is a decision you will always be grateful for.

The top 10 FATAL mistakes after 40

Mistake # 1: Doing work that brings no joy or happiness

Who made up the rule that says work should bring misery? Go ahead and add up the hours of working time left in your life. Calculate up to the day you stop breathing, not the day you retire. It's a big number, isn't it?

Now, how will you spend those hours? The choice is yours.

Mistake # 2: Doing work that does not align your abilities and your interests

This is huge. Think about it. If your work does not include an alignment of your abilities and your interests, no wonder you feel burned out.

Better to be interested in something that you don't have abilities in than to work a lifetime at activities you are good at, but have no interest in.

Mistake # 3: Working for someone else

When you are working just to pay the bills or support your family or please your spouse or your parents, you are dying a slow death. Just like the frog in the slowly heating pot, you won't notice at first. You are too busy working day to day to think about it. Of course you love your family and want to help them.

After forty, you have served society's calling. Now it is your turn to finally do what you love. Enlist the help of those around you for support. If you don't, the pot will boil over right before your eyes.

Mistake # 4: Staying in work that is empty out of fear

Many of us fear what might happen if we take a chance. I suggest you instead look at what you have at stake if you don't change — your life!

I can't guarantee you won't die or become homeless if you follow your passion and figure out now how to do what you love. I *can* guarantee, however, that you will live an empty life without happiness if you continue to spend eight to ten hours a day at just a job.

Not only that, your unhappiness will affect everyone around you.

Mistake # 5: Staying in a job *just* for the money and the perks and the title

Many people do this. The money is nice. It enables us to buy stuff and stay in debt. The free coffee, or laundry, or discount coupons, or the big office with real wood makes us feel important. The title, of course, helps us tell people what we do.

The problem with this strategy is we avoid learning who we are.

When we really find out who we are, we have a much better story to tell ourselves and those around us.

Mistake # 6: Working in a job that does not align with what is most important to you

What is most important to you in your life? Is it your work?

The bigger the gap between your daily activity and what is most important to you, the greater the opportunity for emptiness, a quick death, or even worse, *retirement*.

Mistake # 7: Waiting for permission

If you wait for permission to change and do the work you love, you will have a long wait.

Permission must come from within you. It is not easy, but it is the only way to an authentic life.

Mistake # 8: Becoming comfortable but not happy at work

You know the signs. You know exactly when the boss's report is due each week; you look forward to the Friday night after-work social hour, and the Christmas bonus.

Deep inside, however, you know you are fooling everyone but yourself. The first step towards change is acknowledging the inner signal and doing something about it.

Mistake # 9: Waiting for retirement to be happy

So much can happen between now and retirement, and it will. The only people who retire are people who don't love their work.

Want to slow down the aging process? Do what you love now.

Mistake # 10: Deciding to pursue happiness outside of work

I hear this one all the time. "I can have fun doing what I love on the weekends."

The problem with this strategy is your quality of life declines with this move. Eight to ten hours of working in an empty job, or worse, an empty career, leaves you with very little energy left over for anything fun.

The other day someone asked me how often I worked, and for how many hours. It was such a strange question for me. I didn't know what to say. It was like asking me, how often do I breathe?

Years ago, I did give a numerical answer, of course, but not anymore.

So how about you? Are you working? Or are you breathing life and all that it has to offer?

The next 10 steps to save your life

Save your life?

After forty we tend to be more aware of the time we have remaining, and the things that are still undone in our lives.

While it usually takes a crisis for us to become more aware, a crisis doesn't always motivate us to make changes in our lives, especially in areas that are no longer bringing joy and meaning.

The mid-life crisis can come in a big or a small package. Illness, divorce, layoff, and the death of a loved one are big packages. Daily boredom, unease, sadness, unhappiness, or even depression are simply signs that something is no longer working in our life.

After age forty — at any age, really — it is critical to pay attention to these inner signals.

Here are the ten critical steps you must take now to redesign your life for more joy, happiness, and meaning.

1. **Stop working.**

   That's right; you read this correctly. Stop working and start living. Living with daily joy, happiness, and purpose is worth striving for. It is enjoyable and refills the water glass of life with more energy, more passion, and more excitement.

   Start by finding new work that feels like a better alignment of what you are truly interested in. You may already have the abilities, but if not, you can learn them.

   Many people continue to work at things they are good at, but no longer interested in.

2. **Find some greater purpose.**

   Identify and find something you feel strongly about, or that bothers you about the world, and do something about it.

   It bothers me, for example, that in America we are spending billions of dollars in needless wars while our own cities fall apart. We are now a nation of have and have-nots when it comes to medical care. Our educational system is deeply flawed with too much focus on scores and grades and little focus on learning; besides, education is too costly as well.

   Pick something that really bothers you and build a life purpose around it. Your life will never be the same.

3. **Stand up for your beliefs.**

   Don't be afraid to finally live your life through your causes.

Drive yourself through internal reward rather than external recognition. Replace old beliefs that are no longer useful with new ones that serve you.

4. **Be resilient.**

   Stay focused. Strive for more happiness in your life. Make this a goal in itself. Be selfish and define for yourself what being happy really means to you.

   Despite the barriers and hurdles we must all cross on the journey to more meaning and fulfillment in our lives, keep this vision clear at all times.

5. **Stay organized and structured.**

   Have a plan for your life. This includes your daily living and your long term goals.

   Without a plan for your life that includes your clear intent, when the crisis hits — and it will — your personal roadmap and plan will get you through.

6. **Surround yourself with love.**

   There is no need to have a lonely life.

   Surround yourself with the people you love. If necessary, find new people to love and receive love from. Build relationships that nurture and support your personal roadmap.

7. **Learn to accept your mistakes.**

   I know: This is easier said than done. We are good at beating ourselves up when things go wrong, and we seldom take the time to reflect when things go well.

   Learn to be your own best friend. Learn to accept yourself as you are. Ask yourself;

what can I learn from this experience? What new wisdom can I gain from my actions?

Realize that everything you do or did was done for a good reason at the time. Learn to love yourself more and others will love you more, too.

8. **Don't let the mundane slow you down.**

    Yes, laundry has to be washed, cars need gas, lunches need to be made, and bills need to be paid.

    Ensure that, each and every day, you identify the most important actions you must take to move you towards what you want rather than what you do not want in your life.

9. **Take care of your body and mind.**

    Eat well, sleep well, and exercise daily. Take time each day to reflect on your feelings and thoughts.

    Heard this before? Well, it works. When our bodies and minds are stressed, we lose sight of our goals and what is most important to us in our lives.

    Writing is a good way to reflect on how you are doing. Start a daily journal: Just before bed; answer this question, and write down the answer; "What did I learn today about myself and others?"

10. **Seek joy, not pain.**

    Realign your life and your work around the sole purpose of acquiring more joy, meaning, and happiness in your life. This is in abundance in the world.

Redesign your life with the intent to create more joy for yourself.

Mid-life crisis?

Refocus your attention now on what would be perfect for you in your life. Create a new vision and take small steps each and every day with the intent of creating more joy in your life.

This will make your crisis feel like a crusade. This is a good thing.

How you can live an authentic life

Have you ever asked yourself if you are living the life you were meant to live?

Have you ever asked yourself, as you pondered your life, "Is this all there is?"

These are great questions to ask when you reach forty and beyond.

Who needs an authentic life?

If you are satisfied with the status quo life that no longer challenges you or gives you inspiration and passion, then you don't need an authentic life.

(But, ask yourself: "Am I *really* satisfied with it?")

What is an authentic life?

This is another good question. We rarely teach children or adults how to live an authentic life.

You are living an authentic life if you feel you are in control and you are determining your own direction. Your work is a natural outlet for your creativity, your interests, and your abilities.

Why is living an authentic life important?

We are living longer than ever before. One hundred years ago we wouldn't even be having this conversation since the average person lived barely forty-five years.

There are more opportunities than ever before to re-create our lives and our work.

When we work without purpose and without meaning, our lives become empty and lifeless. Each day is just like the previous day, and the cycle continues until we retire and die. We live for tomorrow; just two more years, or six more years, or ten more years at our miserable jobs until we've saved enough money to finally stop.

When we can finally stop, we're not sure what we will do, but we know it won't be anything like what we are doing now. Then sadly, life gets in the way, and something happens to block our hopes and dreams of a more fulfilling life.

How to build the support network you'll need

Look around you now. Do you have people in your life who support your dreams, your goals, and your daily activities every day? Do these people make you laugh, make you smile, and help you feel better about yourself? Are these people able to truly listen to your needs, especially when it comes to your work?

Many of us start to question our work after we turn forty, and it can seem threatening to those around us. Think about all the years you left early in the morning for work, and came home late at night. You made a good income and never seemed to complain much. Why the sudden need to change *now*, at your age?

This is exactly the time when change is needed most. While most jobs and organizations are only concerned about productivity and being effective, those over forty want more freedom, meaning, and clarity in their work. We want to know *why* we are doing the work, and what difference it is making for our lives, and in the greater world.

With the right support network, new ideas can flourish, new dreams can become real, and new energy for life becomes available.

What happens without the right support network?

People go under. They bury their dreams for "someday" (that never comes). They convince themselves to continue doing the same old routine work, and hope that, by some magic, a good fairy will show up with a wand and make things better.

When you are honest with yourself, you know this won't happen.

Should you fire those around you?

You might have to. Does your support network help you move forward towards what you want, or does it hold you back?

If the people in your life are holding you back, you will need a new team. If the people holding you back happen to be your immediate family, then you must convene an urgent meeting. In this meeting you must tell them you are in a crisis.

Through much reflection, you have discovered that your work no longer fits you. It is time for a new direction. Ask for support and understanding.

You explain that, with or without that support, you must go forward with your new ideas and plans. Let them know that if you don't, you are sure you will die sooner than you planned. Explain that you will do your best to minimize the impact, but you expect that changes will be required.

In the short term, there won't be as much money available, and the whole family will need to downscale the financial requirements of life to accommodate this next journey.

If you find you do not have the support you need, you will have to deal with it sooner or later. I suggest that you set a date within twelve months to do this.

Take the first steps now to build the network you need

You cannot make the changes you need in isolation — you need support. Building a support network can provide you with the help you will need to attain your goals.

Consider thinking of your support network as a series of three tiers. I touched on this earlier, but here is the detailed plan.

A three-tier approach

The bottom tier is made up of "interested" people.

These are people you know are interested in your work. It feels good just being around them. You should have fifteen to twenty of these people in your network

People in the second tier are your "supporters." These are the people who not only take interest in your work, but also come up with ideas to help move you forward. You should have six to ten of these people in your network.

People in the first tier are your "believers." This tier includes your most active supporters. These people provide tangible assistance and bring new referrals and new ideas. A couple of these folks are a great asset.

Start to make a list of new people you could meet, or network with, or both, who are interested in the same things you are interested in (your passions). Make sure you stay in touch with them weekly. You can meet these people in your neighborhood, in online discussion groups, or at networking events.

Make a second list of people who are both interested and supportive of what you want to do. These people will bring you ideas as you start your journey. You want three people who are not only doing what you want to do, but who are also willing to give you ideas and resources to help on your journey. You can take a class, buy a product, sign up for a newsletter — there are many activities that will help you meet these people and get these ideas.

The third step is to find someone who believes in you and your work. This is a person who you might have to pay initially, but who does what you love to do, has great ideas and maybe products you could use, and — most importantly — sends you business.

This is a person who becomes your mentor, your friend, your coach — someone who is interested in your welfare and your success.

What about those you fired?

You won't have time to worry about the old team because you will be too busy building your new team.

At this stage you won't be looking back. You will have begun to build your new life and your new work.

What's at stake?

When you start to take action, you will have new passion and new purpose for your life, and those in it. You will cherish each day and completely use each one.

The best way to get started and build momentum is with the efforts of a new team — a new support network.

Give yourself permission now to follow your heart

Giving yourself permission is harder than you might think. There are many obstacles to cross before doing the work you love. These include financial concerns, relationship concerns, and family concerns — the list seems endless.

Your life is not endless

At forty, we suddenly realize that our life has a finite length. So what better time could there be to create a more fulfilling and meaningful second half of your life?

Look at yourself as a product

There is no product you'll feel better about selling than you.

What are your best features? Who would benefit from using your best features? Who is the best audience for your services or products or both?

The tough part

Actually giving yourself permission will be the toughest part.

Why? We don't usually do it. Perhaps just asking yourself what you are grateful for in your life might lend a new perspective.

It might just save your life

One night years ago I was driving home from teaching my college class. Going down a steep hill very fast, a sudden, overwhelming sadness came over me. I felt empty. This particular night I was driving home with no money and just enough gas to make it home. My kids were waiting for me in our new 400 square foot apartment. There was very little furniture, but much love in the house.

I had placed the car in neutral down the hill to save gas. I thought to myself, "What if my students knew this?"

I felt paralyzed. The divorce, one son in residential treatment for a drug addiction, the suicide of my father less than two years before, the custody battle that took every last dollar, bankruptcy, house foreclosure, cancer scare, the loneliness; these were just a few of my challenges at the time.

For what seemed like minutes, but was probably only a split-second, I felt my hand starting to steer the car to the right and I pondered going over the cliff.

I had never had this thought before. Suddenly I thought: *Who would be there to help my son through his difficult challenge?* Who would be there for my daughter in college and her wonderful daily calls home for more money? And the special time with my youngest son. Where would our special weekends go? And what about a future relationship with someone to love and give love to? And my students, my clients, and their challenges? What about those who would benefit from my ongoing work?

I decided right there that my life was worth living, and I was suddenly grateful for the rich life I did have, despite my current challenges.

In that split-second, I gave myself permission to live.

I can't help thinking that my father might still be alive today if he had thought about what he had to be grateful for, and had found a passion for the second half of his life.

Ten steps for moving forward with your dreams

1. Talk about your vocational passion with others.
2. Build the life you want into your daily routine.
3. Start with five minutes a day to make it a habit.
4. Make your dream a priority each and every day.

5. Study others who are living the life you seek.
6. Celebrate your progress.
7. Have a quiet confidence.
8. Get enough sleep, enough exercise, and eat healthy foods.
9. Have fun and enjoy the process.
10. Become the person you are!

Give yourself permission now; it may save your life.

The Booklet Queen and new fulfillment

1991 was a pivotal mid-forties year in Paulette Ensign's life. Her professional organizing business was almost a decade old. The sales cycle was getting longer and longer for workshop and consulting work, and Paulette continued in these crazy habits called eating and paying the rent.

That's when Paulette spotted an offer for a free booklet called "117 Ideas for Better Business Presentations." She could do business presentations, and the price was right. Her first reaction was, "Gee, I could knock something like this out about organizing tips." Then she threw it in a drawer.

Six months later sitting in her office, bored, baffled, and beaten down by the slow economy, that booklet came to mind. Paulette decided to produce a booklet of organizing tips. She had to shift gears from what had become an uninspiring organizing business.

All those organizing pearls she had shared with clients and seminar audiences about getting organized went into a computer file. The goal was to create a booklet of business organizing tips — a sixteen-page tips booklet that fit into a number 10 business envelope.

Paulette created the booklet — it was called "110 Ideas for Organizing Your Business Life." There was no indication of where this might be heading — Paulette just knew it was time for a change.

The first sales efforts for the booklet were single-copy sales through publicity excerpts in magazines. That became very satisfying as a tub of envelopes, each one containing money, began appearing at the post office. But that was the beginning. Other increasingly rewarding things happened:

A public seminar company contracted Paulette to record an audio program based on the booklet, which led to a twenty-minute interview on a major airline's in-flight audio programming during November and December one year.

A manufacturer's representative decided to send the booklets to his customers rather than his usual calendar. This resulted in the sale of 5,000 imprinted copies, each containing Paulette's contact information.

And then companies started to hire Paulette to write booklets for them, and paid speaking engagements followed, contracted from people who bought the booklets.

A major consumer mail order catalog company licensed a quarter of a million copies of the booklet.

The booklet was licensed for sale in Spanish, Italian, and Dutch, and by manufacturers of other information products into their format in English.

The booklet is also sold in digital format and is downloadable from Paulette's website.

All these activities and more prompted the creation of an entirely new company, one that teaches people to transform their own knowledge into tips booklets and other information products. Each year something new has been added. A website, ezine, and blog were all developed to continuously provide information about writing, producing, and marketing tips booklets.

Paulette created home study kits, she delivers teleclasses by phone, in-person workshops throughout the year, and she now has a thriving consulting practice.

She has had the joy and honor of bringing this work to clients around the world by telephone and in person. There's nothing more fulfilling and rewarding than to see the creative light bulb come on in peoples' lives, and be a catalyst for their success, and their own shift to a more satisfying life.

Clients surpass Paulette's own results by selling over a million copies of their booklets, without spending a penny on advertising. Paulette and her clients all learned plenty together since the original organizing booklet was written in 1991.

The organizing business lived the life it was meant to, bringing many rewards until it was time to recycle the experiences and move on.

Paulette never could have written a business plan for how this unfolded. Paulette *put it all together*, giving herself permission to live the life she created.

And because these career activities are so location-independent, Paulette made a cross country move from New York to southern California in 1996, leaving snow and humidity behind. To say that the move was fulfilling would be gross understatement.

The Art Coach meets the Vocational Coach

Roberta Carasso had been the first and only training coordinator for over seventeen years at a large corporation that had changed hands three times.

Then she did the computer work for a major California county. Increasingly, the county took over her duties and at the time of the introduction of Internet searching, the bureaucracy had changed her work until it became extremely confining, limited in scope, and without room to grow, give an opinion, make a decision, or have any say in what she was doing.

Roberta was well-liked and respected, but the job was pared down to only writing routine weekly, monthly, and yearly reports. Any hope of the creativity she was once allowed was completely gone.

Roberta had a rich and varied past — she had been trained in the arts, she held three degrees and she had been an artist, an art teacher and lecturer, and a responsible program director at the oldest art center in the US, working with major area museums. She had also begun to write, and she had developed a reputation for her expertise.

However, divorce and the need to earn a better salary to support three teenage boys made it necessary to get a "real" job, and that's when Roberta shifted from art education to computer education.

She loved teaching computer classes, but after several years, her employer closed its doors on training.

One thing led to another, and she found herself in her current dead-end position in the municipal bureaucracy. In her fifteenth year, two years prior to her major vocational shift, several artists Roberta had written about asked her to help them with their careers, and her little after-work business, the Art Coach, began to take shape.

Roberta knew she needed to learn to be a better business woman because she saw that growing the business and realizing her passion would be a dream come true.

Timing really is everything — soon Roberta was laid off. Now she could really become the Art Coach.

Although the business is small, Roberta likes it that way. Also, being the boss and not having to answer to anyone else, has brought out the best in Roberta, although it is also a source of some anxiety. She knows she can run a business and make good decisions, but there are stressful times, particularly when she needs to be strong with difficult or demanding people.

But all this is an advantage, too. These experiences are giving Roberta confidence because she is becoming clear about what is important to her and to the success of her artists and her business.

Currently, Roberta works with about twelve artists. She has developed three tracks: 1) career guidance for beginning artists, meeting once or twice, 2) long term contracts where she helps artists get their art exhibited in galleries and museums, and 3) short term work for experienced artists to get their art exhibited in galleries and museums.

Roberta has also begun to network and work with artists in Italy, France, and England.

Artists do need a lot of help, and there are very few people who do what Roberta does. Artists need guidance. Working alone in their studios, they need someone mature, realistic, and experienced to advise them.

As the Art Coach, Roberta helps artists exhibit their passions, their art. Like being an artist, it can be difficult, even lonely at times. But along with her writing, it is very satisfying. No two days are alike; no two artists are alike. The variety of the challenges is invigorating.

Lessons to learn

When we are open to new possibilities, new creativity can emerge and take over, leading you to a more fulfilling life. It takes a little proof for you to see that this new vision can be made real, if only you give yourself permission to start.

We all have special gifts, like Paulette and Roberta, just waiting to emerge and bloom. The problem is that most people wait for someone else to plant the seeds and do the watering. Living an authentic life must come from within you. You must do the planting and watering.

This is the only way you can develop your full confidence, and start living life with integrity and authenticity.

It starts and ends with permission to live your life of joy and happiness. This can start with your work. In mid-life there are no shortcuts to vocational passion. Perhaps this is why so many people quit and just retire, hoping for someday or someone to rescue them from a life void of passion and pleasure.

This does not have to be you. Take the steps yourself, and you, too, can become a role model, showing others a new way of living and thriving after forty.

Putting it all together

How can I live a more fulfilling life?

I developed the simple Ten P Process™ over seven years ago to help people, especially those over forty, discover and do the work they love.

During the last seven years, through workshops, teaching, talks, and private coaching, I have seen this model applied and used by many people on the way to a more authentic life.

It's time for you to follow the steps of the Ten P model, and make the necessary changes in your own life.

Let's recap the 10 P model:

Purpose

What is your life about? How will you make a difference in the world?

What bothers you about the world or your neighborhood, and how can you contribute to solving it through your work? What work could you do that would give you more daily energy and passion? With Purpose, you will experience a greater sense of integrity and authenticity.

Prize

What is most important to you; what do you prize?

Too often we are afraid to admit the answer — too afraid that we will be judged by our decisions rather than by who we are.

Are you working today in a job that has nothing to do with what is most important to you?

If you love teaching, for example, and your days are spent balancing financial statements, only you can do something about it.

Define what is most important to you, and think through now what you will have to do to follow what is most important to you.

Write down specific goals that align with what you prize. This can be a lonely exercise, but the most important one you will ever do.

Perspective

What is your view of yourself? Are you happy with your life, your choices, and your work? What is your view of the world? Does your world inspire you and bring you energy? What is your perspective of others? Do other people interest you, and arouse your curiosity?

Much of our activity in the world revolves around strictly monetary pursuits, and land and political interests. I believe this is a result of people not taking the time to follow a more authentic life that honors their own needs and wants, a life that also honors others and the world they live in.

You can be different; it starts with you.

Possibilities

Have you given up on yourself, or have you started to think of what is possible for you and your work?

It's easy to let others influence your life's direction by telling you what *they* think is impossible. You also need to listen to your own language. Does it inspire you or depress you?

Don't settle for "One day ..." or "I hope ..." or "Maybe if I could ..."

Start now to shape more possibilities for yourself.

For example, imagine a new possibility for yourself and your work right now. Notice how this thought brings on a new thought, and then another and another.

Place

What is your place or role in the world? Have you thought about this?

Have you just assumed that what you do today is the role you are destined to carry out for the rest of your life?

We are all conditioned by our environment, culture, economic situation, and the personality we were born with. These are all hard to change even if you got good grades in school and awards at the office. It will take disciplined effort on your part to think through the roles you want to play in life. No one will do this for you.

Position

What is your position or attitude on a daily basis?

How do you think about yourself, your work, your world, and those around you? Do you wake up daily being grateful or jealous? Do you wake up angry at yourself, your work, and those around you?

Your daily position will either support you and nourish you, or prevent you from enjoying the moment — it will also prevent you from moving towards what you want.

What can you do now to change what is not working each day with regards to your attitude, especially towards your work?

Your daily position will make all the difference.

Passion

Have you ever gone to sleep at night tossing and turning with the excitement of waking up in the morning because you can't wait to get started on your work?

This is vocational passion, and it is one of the most exciting feelings in the world. You are spending your days doing what you love, and your work creates meaning for you.

Make a list of all your passions. Now envision how you could spend your day using these same passions in your work.

Perfect Vocational Day

What would be perfect for you and your work?

Most of us settle for so much less. We hope that if we work harder and faster, the boss will notice us and perhaps we'll get those four days off next winter, or that bonus, or maybe that promotion. With the promotion, we will get to work even harder and faster doing more of what we don't like.

Seems silly, doesn't it?

Spend some time today thinking deeply about, and writing down, exactly what an average day might be like for you if it revolved around your passions.

Present

What are you doing now to close the gap between living an authentic life and your life today?

If you don't know where you are going, then any old road will do. Write down what you want, and compare it to where you are right now.

If there is no gap between these two realities, there will be no tension and no problem.

But if there is a gap, and you need to make changes, your road will not be an easy one. You will encounter emotional challenges. You may have to change some of your beliefs. There will be relationship challenges, and you may have to change some of your relationships. There will be financial challenges, and you may have to make some changes in how you spend your money.

Permission

Putting this all together starts with the right support network.

Start surrounding yourself with people who encourage you, and believe in you, and who provide daily inspiration and ideas about what you want to do.

Look for defining moments in your life. Use these as the trigger to finally live an authentic life, starting with doing the work you love.

Give yourself permission now to follow your heart.

Are you waiting for Life's permission to do what you love?

Is this your story, too?

Work starts out for most of us as something we didn't want to do. We do it to make an income, because we are supposed to, or because we don't know what else to do.

Soon many of us learn that each day is pretty similar to the next. We have little control over what we do, and at times we feel like robots. As we get a little older, we start to wonder, "Is this all there is?" We notice during our long commute how similar all the commuters look. No one is smiling, everyone seems in a rush, and everyone seems permanently attached to their cell phones, pagers, laptops, and palm pilots.

Monday is the worst. Tuesday seems a little better. Wednesday is the longest day because Thursday and Friday still remain. Thursday is not too hot either, because it feels like all the work has to get done today. Friday comes with mixed feelings. Everyone relaxes as if to say, "I don't have to work that hard today, do I? After all, it's Friday!"

It almost feels like a crime to have to work on Fridays. After all, we just spent four whole days doing things we don't like — isn't that enough?

I didn't mention the evenings. We have the usual share of late meetings, overtime, and arriving home late with just enough time to eat and crash on the sofa. Anyone else in our lives who demands attention just has to wait. An important talk with a loved one, taking out the garbage, and the game of Candyland seem so hard to focus on.

Well, back to Friday. Talk fills the office about what everyone has planned for the coming weekend.

Sometimes, when you have nothing planned, it feels like something is missing. After all, everyone else is going away for the weekend.

Not you. You have laundry, cleaning, errands, kids' activities, bills, and most of all, sleep.

This is the weekend you commit to yourself you will finally start to exercise.

When the alarm sounds at six o'clock in the morning on Saturday, the most exercise you feel like doing is reaching over to turn the alarm off.

And before you know it, Sunday night is here again. Great! Time to start worrying about work again.

I hate Monday mornings, you think to yourself. You start fantasizing that suddenly you feel sick, and what it might be like if you called in sick and instead spent the day on the couch with the TV guide in one hand and a drink in the other hand.

Then you suddenly wake up from your dream and realize it is still Monday morning.

You rush around the house, and trip over the shoe left in the middle of the room. You wonder again why you didn't take the time Sunday night to figure out what you would wear — once again you can't find clean underwear or socks that match.

You jump into your car, and as you drive to work you ponder how it would feel if you suddenly got a flat tire and had no choice but to return home.

You start to think about all the meetings and work you must do today as you reach the company parking lot. You feel like you have already worked the whole day.

You walk into the office and everyone you see asks you how your weekend went. This whole ritual takes thirty minutes and by the time you have settled down with a cup of coffee, the boss calls. He wants to see you in his office right away. Something about the missing report that was due last week. *Oh no,* you think to yourself, *that was something I was planning to finish by getting up earlier on Monday morning.*

How could I have done it, you wonder? You were too busy trying to find socks and underwear.

You reach your boss's office, wishing you had the report rather than the underwear and matching socks.

A better way

I have some good news…At mid-life your vocational life doesn't have to be this way.

While most of us start off this way, you can take control of your vocational life.

You can strive to match your abilities and interests so that what you do each and every day fills you with energy, passion, and a sense that what you are doing makes a difference to you and those around you.

Work doesn't have to be a prison sentence. It can be transformed into a lifelong activity that fills you with joy, purpose, and love. That's right — the "L" word.

Yes, it is possible to actually love what you do.

Each day, you awake with a bounce in your step and a smile on your face as you approach your day.

Are you working hard? Sure, but suddenly it doesn't feel that way. You feel like you are on a mission to do more of what you love each and every day.

Monday becomes your best day of the week, and Friday — well, Friday reminds you that you'll have to wait until Monday to continue what you are working on. But you can't wait to get back to it, and over the weekend, you find yourself excited as you sneak thoughts of Monday and what you get to do.

During the week, you feel like laughing out loud and shouting, "This is what work is supposed to feel like!"

But then again, you have lost the concept of work. You feel like this is a vocation that can last a lifetime. Why retire, you ask yourself?

You think to yourself, *Maybe one day, when I am very old, I will slow down a bit, but not too much. After all, this is what I love to do, so why stop?*

Suddenly all this focus on retirement seems sort of silly. After all, retire from what? Doing what I love each and every day?

Maybe that's what retirement ought to be. Going back to what you don't want, if by then you haven't found what you do want. That would be the penalty.

Sadly, that is retirement for most of us.

Taking that first step helps....

As you trudge to the boss's office, you remember long ago reading a book about the concept of vocational passion. At the time, while it sounded interesting, you just couldn't relate. After all, you had bills to pay and you didn't have the time or the opportunity to think about it, much less do what you actually wanted. In your mind back then, doing what you enjoyed and making money seemed an unlikely combination.

Now you smile as you remember this.

Back then, all those P's you read about in the book seemed to be just one more thing to either memorize or ignore forever. Purpose, prize, perspective, possibilities, place, position, passion, perfect vocational day, present and giving permission seemed like a nice model for someone else...

But now at mid-life, you realize that if you can give yourself permission, you can change. With new permission to follow your dreams, your energy can return. Suddenly, you begin to notice that the bounce in your step has started to return, and though you are still working to close the gaps between what you want and where you are, working and waiting to close those gaps doesn't seem all that difficult anymore.

Now as you approach the boss's office without the required report, you smile as you turn the doorknob and you think to yourself, *At least I have my matching socks and my underwear. I'll be OK now that I have given myself permission to do more of what I want.*

Final thoughts

It is my hope that *Don't JUST Retire and Die* has brought you new ideas, new hope, and inspiration.

The road ahead will be challenging, but it will also bring you the most joy and fulfillment you have ever experienced in your life.

You have put in your time, and you deserve a happier life filled with more energy, more fun, and more time with those you love.

All of this is possible when you focus on doing work that fits you just right. Your outlook will change and your world will never be the same. An authentic life awaits you.

When you follow your passions, those around you will benefit from your new life, too. This is the best gift you can offer others — to role model an authentic life for others — don't wait.

I'll be cheering you on as you go.

References and resources

Bateson, G. *Steps to an Ecology of Mind.* New York: Ballantine Books, 1972.

Beebe, John. *Integrity in Depth.* Texas A&M University Press, 1992.

Becker, E. *Birth and Death of Meaning.* New York: Free Press, 1971.

Becker, *The Denial of Death.* New York: Free Press, 1973.

Campbell, J. *The Hero with a Thousand Faces.* Princeton: Princeton University Press, 1968.

Cochran, L. *The Sense of Vocation.* Albany: State University of New York Press, 1990.

Csikszentmihalyi, M. *Flow.* New York: Harper and Row, 1990.

Deci, E. *Intrinsic Motivation.* New York: Plenum Press, 1975.

Frankl, V. *Man's Search for Meaning.* New York: Simon and Schuster, 1984.

Fromm, E. *On Being Human.* New York: Continuum International Publishing Group, 1994.

Halberstam, J. *Work.* New York: Berkeley, 2000.

Hollis, James. *Finding Meaning in the Second Half of Life.* Gotham Books, a division of Penguin, 2005.

Hollis, James. *The Middle Passage: From Misery to Meaning in Mid-Life.* Inner City Books, 1993

Hollis, James. *Creating a Life: Finding Your Individual Path.* Inner City Books, 2000.

Hyman, Carol. "Can Money Buy Happiness? UC Berkeley Researchers Find Surprising Answers." Media Relations, 16 June, 2003.

James, William. *The Principles of Psychology.* Dover, MA: Dover Publications, 1955.

Jacques, E. *"Death and the Mid-life Crisis."* International Journal of Psychoanalysis, 1965. 41: p. 502-514.

Jung, C. *The Undiscovered Self.* New York: A Mentor Book, 1957.

Kotlikoff, Laurence. "The Nest-egg Philosopher," CNN Money. April 2007.

Leshan, E. *The Wonderful Crisis of Middle Age.* New York: Warner Books, 1973.

Levinson, D. *The Seasons of a Man's Life.* New York: Ballantine Books, 1978.

May, R. *Man's Search for Himself.* New York: Dell, 1973.

May, R. *The Courage to Create*. New York: Bantam Books, 1976.

McAdams, D.P. *The Stories We Live by*. New York: Guilford Press, 1993.

Nathanson, Craig. *P Is for Perfect: Your Perfect Vocational Day*. Ottawa: Book Coach Press, 2003.

Nathanson, Craig. *Discover and Live your Passion 365 Days a Year*. Ottawa: The Sharp Quill, 2005.

Sammon, S. *Life after Youth*. New York: Abba House, 1997.

Skinner, B. F. *Science and Human Behavior*. Simon & Schuster, Inc., 1953.

Craig's biography

Craig Nathanson was very successful in corporate America for over twenty-five years doing all the right things, and following all the right steps. Yet, he was empty inside, good at things he didn't care deeply about.

After several layoffs and a brief, but life-changing bit of introspection, he decided to finally follow his perfect vocational day, which includes teaching, coaching mid-life adults, and writing, combined with daily exercise, healthy eating, and quality time with his family.

Craig Nathanson is now The Vocational Coach, an internationally known author, workshop leader, speaker, college lecturer, and coach for mid-life adults. He is dedicated to guiding individuals to discover and experience their vocational passions in mid-life, while making an income doing what they love.

The change in Craig's life is much more, however, than increased family time and more possibilities to do what he wants to do each day. It is deeper. He has a renewed sense of the world around him, and in his local community. People seem more interesting, there is so much to learn, and the air is fresher to breathe.

As part of Craig's continuing education, he has a Ph.D in Human and Organizational Systems. He currently holds two masters degrees, in Telecommunications Management and Human Development, and an undergraduate degree in Human Relations and Organizational Behavior.

Craig describes his purpose in life to be spirited, compelled, and passionate, enabling those who cross his path to make a difference

Craig lives with his family in Petaluma, California.

www.ingramcontent.com/pod-product-compliance
Lightning Source LLC
Chambersburg PA
CBHW020757160426
43192CB00006B/361